Microsoft Office 365/2016 Keyboard Shortcuts

For Macintosh

By

U. C-Abel Books.

ISBN-13: 978-9785457438
ISBN-10: 9785457435

Published by U. C-Abel Books.

A Summarized Preview of Contents.

Table of Contents

Acknowledgement.

U. C-Abel Books will not take all credits for Microsoft Office 365/2016 keyboard shortcuts listed in this book, but shares it with Microsoft Corporation because some of the shortcuts came from them and are "used with permission from Microsoft".

Dedication

This compilation is dedicated to Mac computer users and lovers of keyboard shortcuts all over the world.

Introduction.

We enjoy using shortcuts because they set us on a high plane that astonishes people around us when we work with them. As wonderful shortcuts users, the worst eyesore we witness in computer operation is to see somebody sluggishly struggling to execute a task through mouse usage when in actual sense shortcuts will help to save that person time. Most people have asked us to help them with a list of keyboard shortcuts that can make them work as smartly as we do and that drove us into research to broaden our knowledge and truly help them as they demanded, that is the reason for the existence of this book. It is a great tool for lovers of shortcuts, and those who want to join the group.

Most times the things we love don't come by easily. It is our love for keyboard shortcuts that made us to bear long sleepless nights like owls just to make sure we get the best out of it, and it is the best we got that we are sharing with you in this book. You cannot be the same at computing after reading this book. The time you entrusted to our care is an expensive possession and we promise not to mess it up.

Thank you.

What to Know Before You Begin.

General Notes.

1. For effective use of keyboard shortcuts listed in this book, JAWS users must turn off Virtual Ribbon Menu feature.
2. Most of the keyboard shortcuts you will see in this book refer to the U.S. keyboard layout. Keys for other layouts might not correspond exactly to the keys on a U.S. keyboard. Keyboard shortcuts for laptop computers might also differ.
3. It is important to note that when using shortcuts to perform any command, you should make sure the target area is active, if not you may get a wrong result. Example, if you want to highlight all texts you must make sure the text field is active and if an object, make sure the object area is active. The active area is always known by the location where the cursor of your computer blinks.
4. On a Mac keyboard, the Command key is denoted with the ⌘symbol.
5. The settings in some versions of the Macintosh operating system and some utility applications might conflict with keyboard shortcuts and function key operations in Office.
6. If a function key doesn't work as you expect it to, press the Fn key in addition to the function key. If you don't want to press the Fn key every time, you can change your Apple system preferences.
7. The plus (+) sign that comes in the middle of keyboard shortcuts simply means the keys are meant to be combined or held down together not to be added as one of the

shortcut keys. In a case where plus sign is needed; it will be duplicated (++).

8. Many keyboards assign special functions to function keys, by default. To use the function key for other purposes, you have to press Fn+the function key.
9. For keyboard shortcuts in which you press one key immediately followed by another key, the keys are separated by a comma (,).
10. It is also important to note that the keyboard shortcuts listed in this book are for Microsoft Office 365/2016 for Mac.

Other Areas to Take Note of.

Common Office For Mac Keyboard Shortcuts

The common office for mac keyboard shortcuts listed in this book are applicable to Excel 2016 for Mac, PowerPoint 2016 for Mac, Word for Mac 2016, Outlook 2016 for Mac, Word for Mac 2011, Excel for Mac 2011, Outlook for Mac 2011, and PowerPoint for Mac 2011.

Create a custom keyboard shortcut for Office 2016 for Mac.

The steps written on how to create a custom keyboard shortcuts for office 2016 for mac applies to all programs included in this book.

Word 2016 For Mac

Keyboard shortcuts listed in this section are for use in Word 2016 for Mac.

OneNote for Mac

Keyboard shortcuts listed in this section are for use in OneNote for Mac 2016.

Excel for Mac

Excel keyboard shortcuts listed in this section are for use in Excel 2016 for Mac. If you use Excel on a Windows computer, many of the shortcuts that use the CTRL key also work in Excel 2016 for Mac. However, not all do. When in doubt, consult this list.

Outlook 2016 for Mac

Outlook keyboard shortcuts listed in this section are for use in Office 365, Office 365 Admin, Office 365 Small Business Admin, and Outlook 2016 for Mac.

PowerPoint 2016 for Mac

Keyboard shortcuts listed in this section are to be used in PowerPoint 2016 for Mac, PowerPoint for Mac 2011, and PowerPoint for iPad.

Some Short Forms You Will Find in This Book and Their Full Meaning.

Here are short forms used in this Microsoft Office 365/2016 Keyboard Shortcuts For Macintosh book and their full meaning.

1. Win - Windows logo key
2. Tab - Tabulate Key
3. Shft - Shift Key
4. Prt sc - Print Screen
5. Num Lock - Number Lock Key
6. F - Function Key
7. Esc - Escape Key
8. Ctrl - Control Key
9. Caps Lock - Caps Lock Key
10. Alt - Alternate Key

CHAPTER 1.

About Office 2016 and Mac.

Introduction to Microsoft Office.

Microsoft Office is a computer software made up of apps, servers and services, developed and marketed by Microsoft Corporation.

Definition of Macintosh.

Macintosh is a popular model of computer manufactured and marketed by Apple Inc. that features a graphical user interface which uses windows, icons, and a mouse to make it relatively easy for newbies/novices to use the computer effectively.

Differences between (Macintosh) Macs and Personal Computers (Pcs). By www.diffen.com

A **PC** generally refers to a computer that runs on the Windows operating system. It is also defined as an IBM-compatible computer, thereby meaning that its architecture is based on the IBM microprocessor. A number of different operating systems are compatible with PCs; the most popular of which is Microsoft Windows. Some others are the UNIX variants, such as Linux, FreeBSD, and Solaris.

On the other hand **Macintosh**, commonly known as **Mac**, is a brand name which covers several lines of personal computers designed, developed, and marketed by Apple Inc. The Mac is the only computer in the world that can run all the major operating systems, including Mac OS X, Windows XP, and Vista. With software like Parallels Desktop or VMware Fusion they can be run; side by side.

Macs and PCs both have dedicated followers, and each type of computer has its own strengths and weaknesses.

Mac		**PC**
What is it?	Short form for "Macintosh" and refers to any computer produced by Apple, Inc.	Refers to any computer running IBM-Based (Windows, Linux, Solaris, FreeBSD) operating systems. stands for "Personal Computer"
Cost	Computers start at $499 for the Mac Mini desktop, $899 for the Macbook Air notebook, and $1099 for the iMac all-in-one. Other models are more expensive. For desktop or home use Macs are generally expensive than a PC.	Compared to a Mac, Windows and Windows-associated hardware is cheaper, and you can build your own for even less money. Comparable computers running Windows can be found around 40% cheaper than a Mac.
Manufacturer	Apple Inc	Several companies: HP,

		Toshiba, Dell, Lenovo, Samsung, Acer, Gateway etc.
Development and Distribution	Macs are developed and distributed by Apple Inc.	PCs are manufactured and distributed by hundreds of manufacturers.
Company / developer	Apple, Inc.	Microsoft (Windows), Ubuntu (Linux), Sun (Solaris), etc.
Gaming	Not as many games are made natively for the Mac, although in recent years, many more applications are released for them. The App Store is a hub for users to download games from.	The library of games available for the PC is exhaustive, and hardware specifically tweaked for gaming performance is much more readily available for Windows. The array of graphics cards and upgradability also favor Windows-based computers.
User	Home users and businesses (mainly in the creative department)	Home users and businesses
Available language(s)	Multilingual	Must purchase a different OS Version, but has multiple languages available.

OS family	Unix-like (BSD>Darwin>Mac)	Windows, Linux, Solaris, FreeBSD, etc.
Popular Applications	Photos, iMovie, GarageBand, Pages, Numbers, Keynote, Safari, Mail, Messages, FaceTime, Calendar, Contacts, App Store, iTunes, iBooks, Maps, Photo Booth, Time Machine	MS Office, Internet Explorer, Media Player, Media Center, Windows Defender, SkyDrive, VLC media player, Chrome browser
Latest Operating System	OS X Yosemite (version 10.10); OS X El Capitan (version 10.11) announced	Windows 8/8.1, Windows 10 announced
Compatibility	Can open almost all PC files and can coexist on local networks with PCs. Can open .doc, .exe (as a compressed bundle), .xls, and others. Software exists for other file types. Can also run Windows on a Mac for 100% compatibility.	Mac-based files (.DMG) cannot be opened on PCs natively, but you can install software that can read, and possibly write Mac-based files on a PC.
Supported architectures	Intel Microprocessors	Intel and AMD processors
Market Reach	Attracts graphic designers, video and music producers, tech journalists, app developers etc.	Wide reach to all stratas. Business users tend to use Windows hardware due to compatibility.
Virus Attacks	Since Macs are not as popular as PCs, there are fewer malware written to target Macs, although the threat of	Being the popular desktop choice, most virus writers target Windows systems, however,

	malicious software is growing, like from Java.	Linux often has less malware.
Compatible Operating Systems	OS X, Windows (through virtual machine or Boot Camp), Linux	Windows, Linux
Performance	Since Apple have controlled the hardware & software bundles and model updates, so every Mac operates smoothly without worry on lagging, incompatibles, and have stable and expected performance	Different OEMs and even custom build PCs might not have the suitable drivers released for every components in each OS version, incompatibles, lagging may occur. Maybe cannot reach expected performance
Repairs	Any knowledgeable person can perform repairs and upgrades. Local computer-help stores can also be contacted for repairs. AppleCare can extend the warranty. Newer Macs are becoming less upgrade-friendly, though.	Any knowledgeable person can perform repairs and upgrades. Local computer-help stores can also be contacted for repairs. OEMs and component shops provides limited warranty.
Programs and apps	Same as gaming, limited choice due to user range.	Same as gaming, excess choice due to user range.
Piracy Prevention	Activation is not required, can reinstall as many times as needed.	Windows has a unique activation key for each package distribution, and lots of custom and

		OEM PC appears, so genuine checking become important. Linux, Solaris, FreeBSD is free and no need for those keys.
Customizability	No	Yes
Messaging	Messages (using iMessage, Google Talk, etc.)	Skype, Facebook, and Twitter
Voice commands	Yes	Yes
Maps	Yes	Yes
Internet browsing	Safari, Chrome, Firefox, plus many more.	Internet Explorer, Chrome, Firefox, Safari (no longer supported)
App store	App Store	Windows Store
Widgets	Yes	Yes
Working state	Current	Current
Interface	Mouse, keyboard, trackpad, other peripherals	Mouse, keyboard, trackpad, other peripherals
Has Registry	No	Yes
Overclockable	No	Yes, depends on CPU and Motherboard

Introduction to Office 2016 for Mac.

Office 2016 is an office suite developed and sold by Microsoft. The preview version of Microsoft Office for Mac was released on 5th March 2015, then the final version was released on 5th July 2015 by Microsoft Corporation.

Supported languages in Office 2016 for Mac

Office 2016 for Mac is currently available in the following languages:

- Arabic
- Brazilian Portuguese
- Chinese (Simplified)
- Chinese (Traditional)
- Czech
- Danish
- Dutch
- English
- Finnish
- French
- Hebrew
- German
- Italian
- Japanese
- Norwegian Bokmal
- Polish
- Russian
- Spanish
- Swedish
- Thai

The Difference between Office 365 and Office 2016.

Office 365 is a subscription service (this means you pay for it on monthly or yearly basis) provided by Microsoft Corporation that includes the most recent version of office, which currently is also called office 2016. Some of the office

365 plans like HOME, let you share your subscription with people around you.

Contrariwise, Office 2016 is marketed as a one-time purchase bundle, this simply means you pay a single upfront cost to receive Office programs/applications for your personal or Macintosh computer. No upgrade option.

The major difference is that Office 365 has an upgrade option while office 2016 doesn't, this means that after you have purchased Office 2016 bundle, you will have to purchase another in future if there is an upgrade (added feature) you desire.

CHAPTER 2.

Fundamental Knowledge of Keyboard Shortcuts.

Without the existence of keyboard, there wouldn't have been anything like keyboard shortcuts so in this chapter we will learn a little about the computer keyboard before moving to keyboard shortcuts.

1. Definition of Computer Keyboard.

This is an input device that is used to send data to computer memory.

Sketch of a Keyboard

1.1 Types of Keyboard.

i. Standard (Basic) Keyboard.
ii. Enhanced (Extended) Keyboard.

i. **Standard Keyboard:** This is a keyboard designed during the 1800s for mechanical typewriters with just 10 function keys (F keys) placed at the left side of it.
ii. **Enhanced Keyboard:** This is the current 101 to 102-key keyboard that is included in almost all the personal computers (PCs) of nowadays, which has 12 function keys at the top side of it.

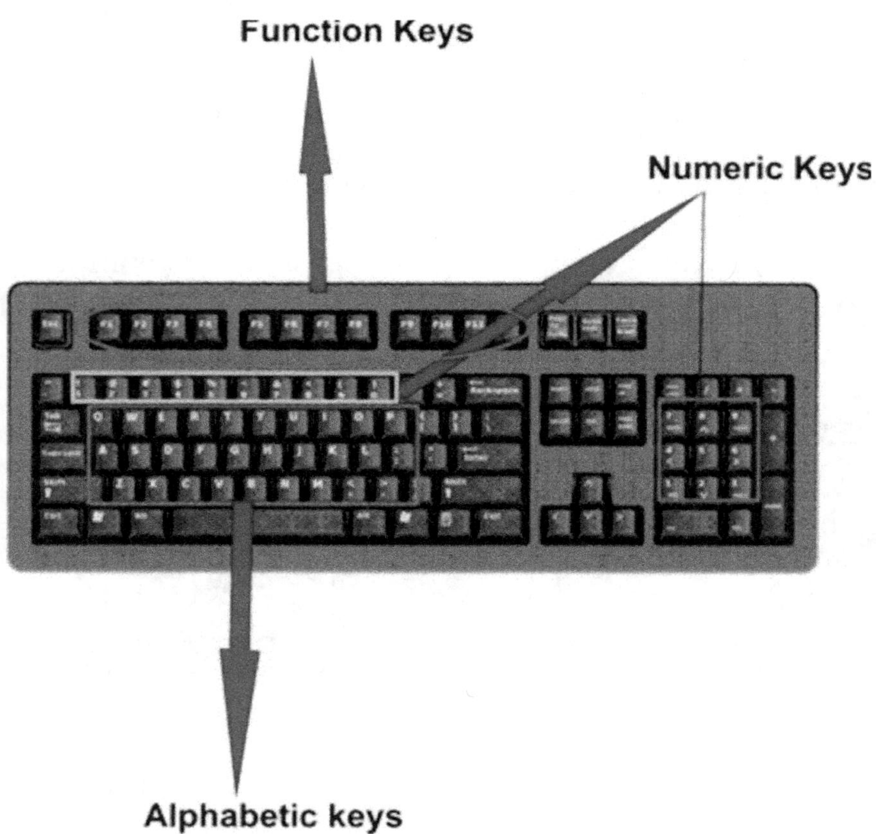

1.2 Segments of the keyboard

- Numeric keys
- Alphabetic keys
- Punctuation keys
- Windows Logo key.
- Function keys
- Special keys

Numeric Keys: Numeric keys are keys with numbers from **0 - 9**.

Alphabetic Keys: These are keys that have alphabets on them, ranging from **A** to **Z**.

Punctuation Keys: These are keys of the keyboard used for punctuation, examples include comma, full stop, colon, question marks, hyphen, etc.

Windows Logo Key: A key on Microsoft Computer keyboard with its logo displayed on it. Search for this on your keyboard.

Apple Key: This also known as Command key is a modifier key that you can find on an Apple keyboard. It usually has the image of an apple or command logo on it. Search for this on your Apple keyboard

Function Keys: These are keys that have **F** on them which are usually combined with other keys. They are F1 - F12, and are also in the class called *Special Keys*.

Special Keys: These are keys that perform special functions. They include: Tab, Ctrl, Caps lock, Insert, Prt sc, alt gr, Shift, Home, Num lock, Esc and many others. Special keys differs according to the type of computer involved. In some keyboard layout, especially laptops, the keys that turn the speaker on/off, the one that increases/decreases volume, the key that turns the computer Wifi on/off are also special keys.

Other Special Keys Worthy of Note.

Enter Key: This is located at the right-hand corner of most keyboards. It is used to send messages to the computer to execute commands, in most cases it is used to mean "Ok" or "Go".

Escape Key (ESC): This is the first key on the upper left of most keyboards. It is used to cancel routines, close menus and select options such as **Save** according to circumstance.

Control Key (CTRL): It is located on the bottom row of the left and right hand side of the keyboard. They also work with the function keys to execute commands using Keyboard shortcuts (key combinations).

Alternate Key (ALT): It is located on the bottom row also of some keyboard, very close to the CTRL key on both side of the keyboard. It enables many editing functions to be accomplished by using some keystroke combinations on the keyboard.

Shift Key: This adds to the roles of function keys. In addition, it enables the use of alternative function of a particular button (key), especially, those with more than one function on a key. E.g. use of capital letters, symbols and numbers.

1.3. Selecting/Highlighting With Keyboard.

This is a highlighting method or style where data is selected using keyboard instead of a computer mouse.

To do this:

- Move your cursor to the text you want to highlight, make sure that area is active
- Hold down the shift key with one finger
- Then use another finger to move the arrow key that points to the direction you want to highlight.

1.4 The Operating Modes Of The Keyboard.

Just like mouse, keyboard has two operating modes. The two modes are Text Entering Mode and Command Mode.

a. **Text Entering Mode:** this mode gives the operator/user the opportunity to type text.
b. **Command Mode:** this is used to command the operating system/software/application to execute commands in certain ways.

2. Ways To Improve In Your Typing Skill.

1. Put Your Eyes Off The Keyboard.

This is the aspect of keyboard usage that many don't find funny because they always ask. "How can I put my eyes off the keyboard when I am running away from the occurrence of errors on my file?" My aim is to be fast, is this not going to slow me down?

Of course, there will be errors and at the same time your speed will slow down but the motive behind the introduction to this method is to make you faster than you are. Looking at your keyboard while you type can make you get a sore neck, it is better you learn to touch type because the more you type with your eyes fixed on the screen instead of the keyboard, the faster you become.
An alternative to keeping your eyes off your keyboard is to use the "*Das Keyboard Ultimate*".

2. Errors Challenge You
It is better to fail than not trying at all. Not trying at all is an attribute of the weak and lazybones. When you make mistakes, try again because errors are opportunities for improvement.

3. Good Posture (Position Yourself Well).
Do not adopt an awkward position while typing. You should get everything on your desk organized or arranged before sitting to type. Your posture while typing contributes to your speed and productivity.

4. Practice
Here is the conclusion of everything said above. You have to practice your shortcuts constantly. The practice alone is a way of improvement. "Practice brings improvement". Practice always.

2.1 Software That Will Help You Improve Your Typing Skill.

There are several Software programs for typing that both kids and adults can use for their typing skill. Here is a list of software that can help you improve in your typing: Mavis Beacon, Typing Instructor, Mucky Typing Adventure, Rapid Tying Tutor, Letter Chase Tying Tutor, Alice Touch Typing Tutor and many more. Personally, I recommend Mavis Beacon.

To learn typing with MAVIS BEACON, install Mavis Beacon software to your computer, start with keyboard lesson, then move to games. Games like ***Penguin Crossing, Creature Lab*** or ***Space Junk*** will help you become a professional in typing. Typing and keyboard shortcuts work hand-in-hand.

Sketch of a computer mouse

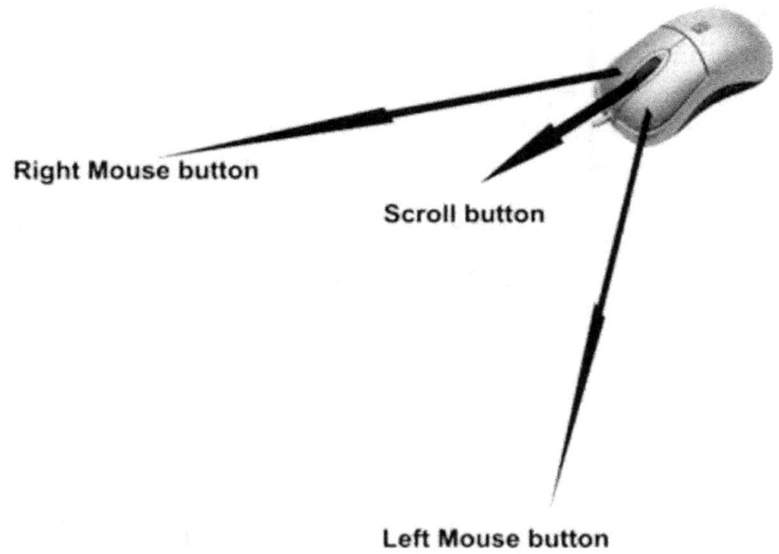

3. Mouse:

This is an oval-shaped portable input device with three buttons for scrolling, left clicking, and right clicking that enables work to be done effectively on a computer. The plural form of mouse is mice.

3.1 Types of Computer Mouse

- Mechanical Mouse
- Optical Mechanical Mouse (Optomechanical)
- Laser Mouse
- Optical Mouse
- BlueTrack Mouse

3.2 Forms of Clicking:

Left Clicking: This is the process of clicking the left side button of the mouse. It can also be called *clicking* without the addition of *left*.

Right Clicking: It is the process of clicking the right side button of a computer mouse.

Double Clicking: It is the process of clicking the left side button two times (twice) and immediately.

Double clicking is used to select a word while thrice clicking is used to select a sentence or paragraph.

Scroll Button: It is the little key attached to the mouse that looks like a tiny wheel. It takes you up and down a page when moved.

3.3 Mouse Pad: This is a small soft mat that is placed under the mouse to make it have a free movement.

3.4 Laptop Mouse Touchpad

This unlike the mouse we explained above is not external, rather it is inbuilt (comes with a laptop computer). With the presence of a laptop mouse touchpad, an external mouse is not needed to use a laptop, except in a case where it is malfunctioning or the operator prefers to use external one for some reasons.

The laptop mouse touchpad is usually positioned at the end of the keyboard section of a laptop computer. It is rectangular in shape with two buttons positioned below it. The two buttons/keys are used for left and right clicking just like the external mouse. Some laptops come with four mouse keys.

Two placed above the mouse for left and right clicking and two other keys placed below it for the same function.

4. Definition Of Keyboard Shortcuts.

Keyboard shortcuts are defined as a series of keys, sometimes with combination that execute tasks that typically involve the use of mouse or other input devices.

5. Why You Should Use Shortcuts.

1. One may not be able to use a computer mouse easily because of disability or pain.

2. One may not be able to see the mouse pointer as a result of vision impairment, in such case what will the person do? The answer is SHORTCUT.

3. Research has made it known that Extensive mouse usage is related to Repetitive Syndrome Injury (RSI) greatly than the use of keyboard.

4. Keyboard shortcuts speed up computer users, making learning them a worthwhile effort.

5. When performing a job that requires precision, it is wise that you use the keyboard instead of mouse, for instance, if you are dealing with Text Editing, it is better you handle it using keyboard shortcuts than spending more time with your computer mouse alone.

6. Studies calculate that using keyboard shortcuts allows working 10 times faster than working with the mouse. The time you spend looking for the mouse and then getting the cursor to the position you want is lost!

Reducing your work duration by 10 times brings you greater results.

5.1 Ways To Become A Lover Of Shortcuts.

1. Always have the urge to learn new shortcut keys associated with the programs you use.
2. Be happy whenever you learn a new shortcut.
3. Try as much as you can to apply the new shortcuts you learnt.
4. Always bear it in mind that learning new shortcuts is worth it.
5. Always remember that the use of keyboard shortcuts keeps people healthy while performing computer activities.

5.2 How To Learn New Shortcut Keys

1. Do a research for them: quick reference (a cheat sheet comprehensively compiled like ours) can go a long way to help you improve.
2. Buy applications that show you keyboard shortcuts every time you execute an action with mouse.
3. Disconnect your mouse if you must learn this fast.
4. Read user manuals and help topics (Whether offline or online).

5.3 Your Reward For Knowing Shortcut Keys.

1. You will get faster unimaginably.
2. Your level of efficiency will increase.
3. You will find it easy to use.

4. Opportunities are high that you will become an expert in what you do.
5. You won't have to go for **Office button**, click **New,** click **Blank and Recent** and click **Create** just to insert a fresh/blank page. **Ctrl +N** takes care of that in a second.

A Funny Note: Keyboarding and Mousing are in a marital union with Keyboarding being the head, so it will be unfair for anybody to put asunder between them.

5.4 Why We Emphasize On The Use of Shortcuts.

You may never ditch your mouse completely unless you are ready to make your brain a box of keyboard shortcuts which will really be frustrating, just imagine yourself learning all shortcuts that go with the programs you use and their various versions. You shouldn't learn keyboard shortcuts that way.

Why we are emphasizing on the use of shortcuts is because mouse usage is becoming unusually common and unhealthy, too. So we just want to make sure both are combined so you can get fast, productive and healthy in your computer activities. All you need to know is just the most important ones associated with the programs you use.

CHAPTER 3.

How to Download, Install, Launch, and Uninstall Office 2016 for Mac.

Download and Install Office 2016 for Mac

1. Go to your **My Account** page at Office.com and sign in with your Microsoft account.
2. On the **My Account** page, under the name of your subscription, select **Install**.

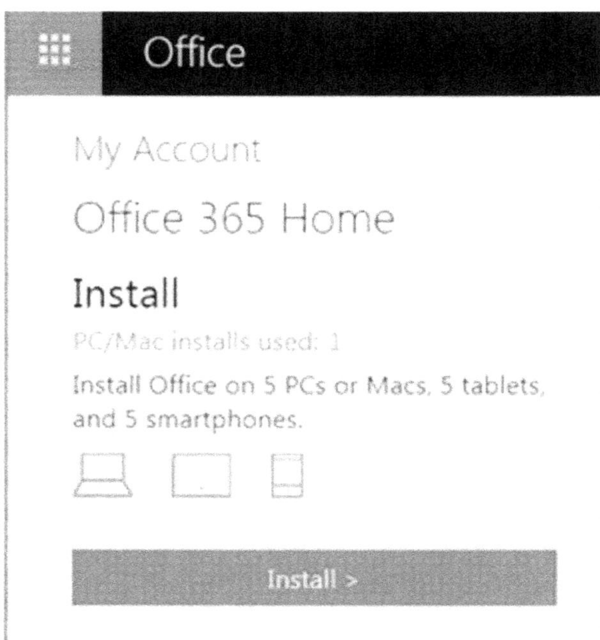

3. On the next page, under **Install information**, select **Install** to begin downloading the installation package.

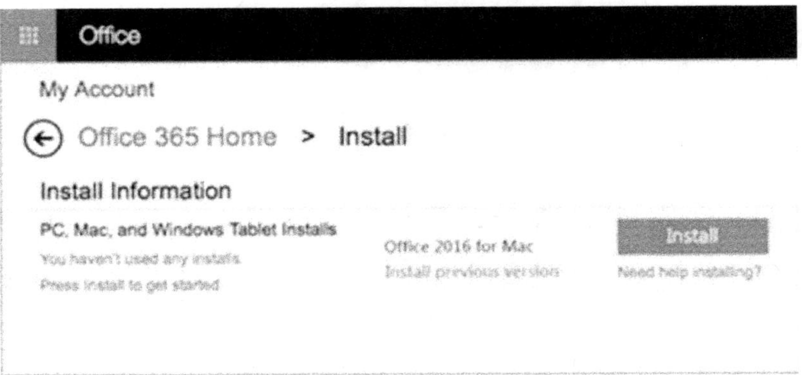

4. Once the download has completed, open Finder, go to **Downloads**, and double-click **Microsoft_Office_2016_Installer.pkg** (the name might vary slightly).

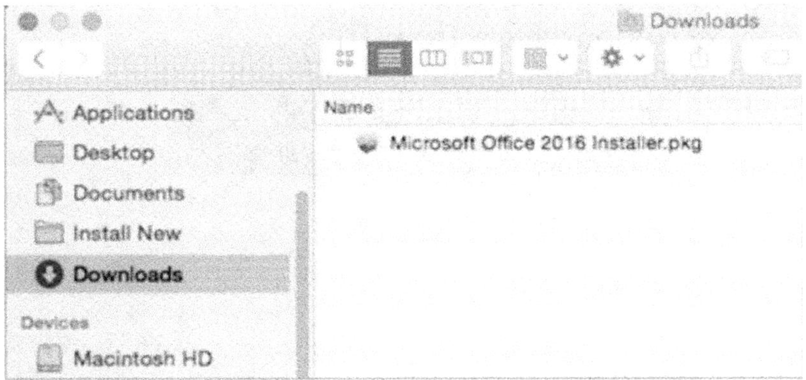

Tip: If you see an error that the Microsoft_Office_2016_Installer.pkg can't be opened because it is from an unidentified developer, wait 10 seconds and then try double-clicking the installer package again. If you are stuck at the **Verifying....** progress bar, close or cancel the progress bar and try again.

5. On the first installation screen, select **Continue** to begin the installation process.

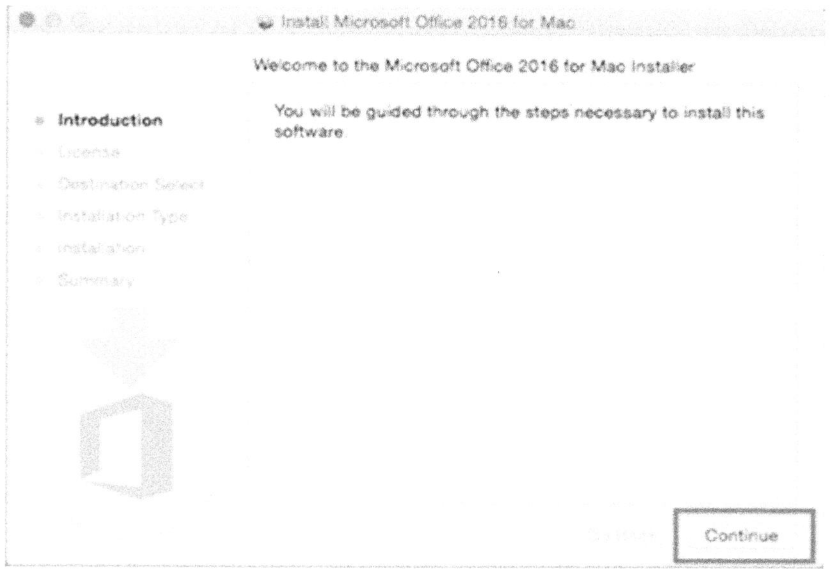

6. Review the software license agreement, and then click **Continue**.
7. Select **Agree** to agree to the terms of the software license agreement.
8. Review the disk space requirements, and then click **Install**.
9. Enter your Mac login password, if prompted, and then click **Install Software**. (This is the password that you use to log in to your Mac.)

10. The software begins to install. Click **Close** when the installation is finished.

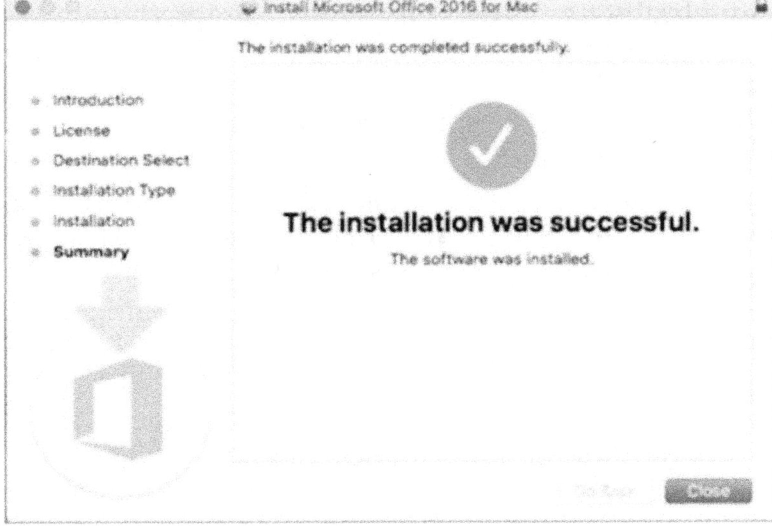

Launch an Office for Mac app and start the activation process.

1. Click the **Launchpad** icon in the Dock to display all of your apps.

2. Click the **Microsoft Word** icon in the Launchpad.

3. The **What's New** window opens automatically when you launch Word. Click **Get Started** to start activating.

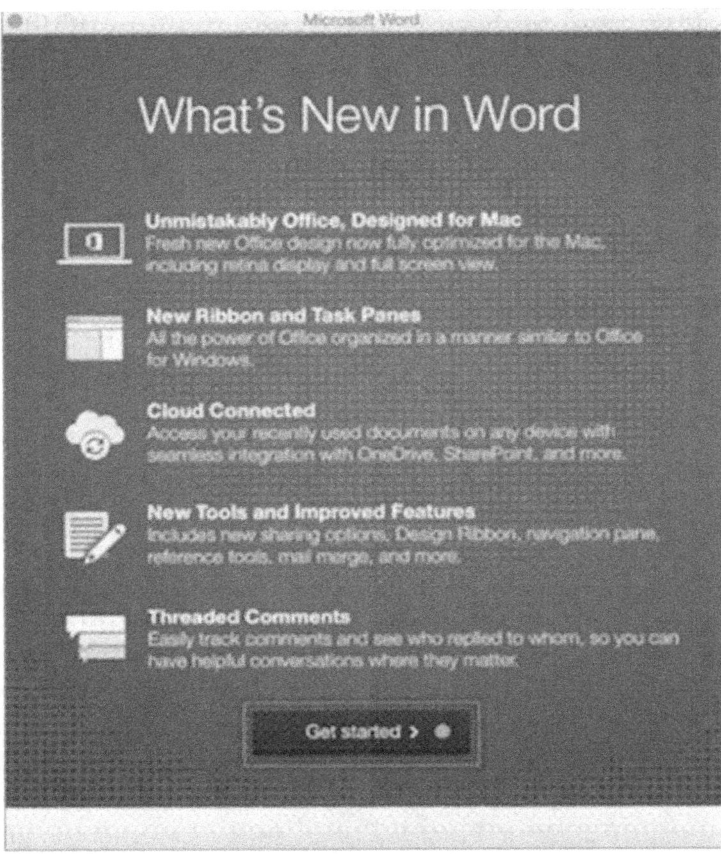

Installation notes

Can I install Office 2016 for Mac and Office for Mac 2011 on the same computer?

Yes, you can install and use Office 2016 for Mac and Office for Mac 2011 at the same time just like Office 2016 and Office 2013 for Windows. However, we recommend that you uninstall Office for Mac 2011 before you install the new version just to prevent any confusion.

How do I pin the Office app icons to the dock?

1. Go to **Finder** > **Applications** and open the Office app you want.
2. In the Dock, Control+click or right-click the app icon and choose **Options** > **Keep in Dock**.

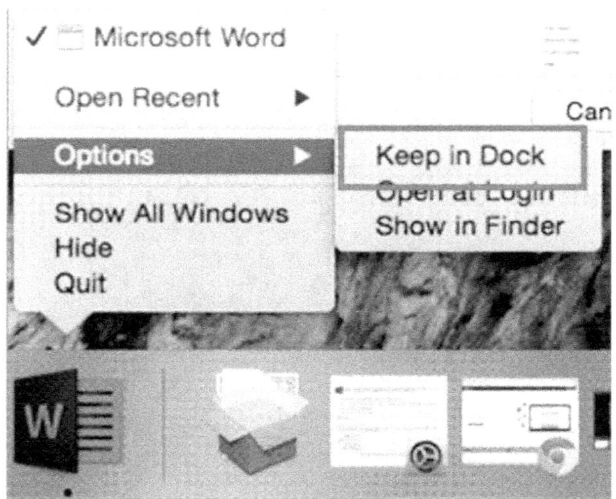

Uninstall Office 2016 for Mac.

Applies To: Excel 2016 for Mac, Outlook 2016 for Mac, PowerPoint 2016 for Mac, Word 2016 for Mac, and OneNote 2016 for Mac.

To uninstall Office 2016 for Mac, move the applications and user preference files to the Trash. Once you've removed everything, empty the Trash and restart your Mac to complete the process.

You must be signed in as an administrator or provide an administrator name and password to complete these steps.

Remove Office 2016 for Mac Applications.

1. Open Finder and click **Applications**.
2. Command ⌘+click to select all of the Office 2016 for Mac applications.
3. Ctrl+click or right-click the applications you selected and click **Move to Trash**.

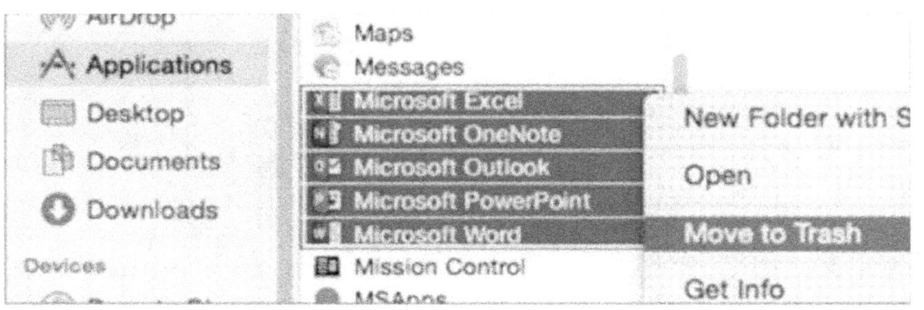

Remove Files from Your User Library Folder.

To remove files from your user **Library** folder, you'll need to first set the Finder View options.

1. In Finder, press ⌘+**Shift+h**.
2. On the Finder menu, click **View** > **as List**, and then click **View** > **Show View Options**.
3. In the **View Options** dialog box, select **Show Library Folder**.

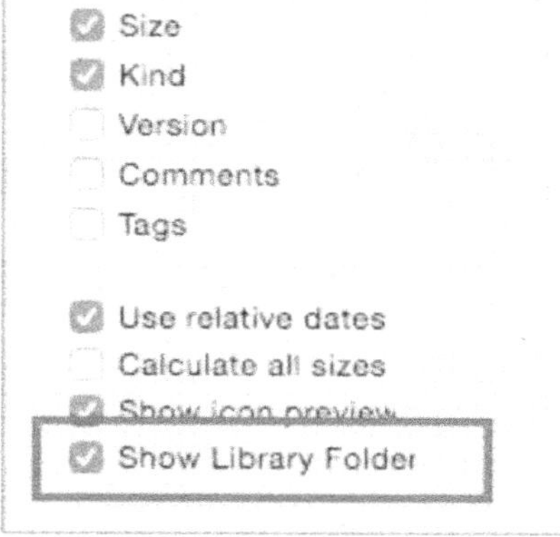

4. Switch back to Column view (⌘+3) and click **<YourUserName>Library** > **Containers** and ctrl+click or right-click each of these folders if present, and then click **Move to Trash**.
    - **com.microsoft.errorreporting**
    - **com.microsoft.Excel**
    - **com.microsoft.netlib.shipassertprocess**
    - **com.microsoft.Office365ServiceV2**
    - **com.microsoft.Outlook**
    - **com.microsoft.Powerpoint**
    - **com.microsoft.RMS-XPCService**
    - **com.microsoft.Word**
    - **com.microsoft.onenote.mac**
5. **Warning:** Outlook data will be removed when you move the three folders listed in this step to **Trash**. You should back up these folders before you delete them.

    Switch back to Column view (⌘+3) and click **<YourUserName>Library** > **Group Containers** and ctrl+click or right-click each of these folders if present, and then click **Move to Trash**.

    - **UBF8T346G9.ms**
    - **UBF8T346G9.Office**
    - **UBF8T346G9.OfficeOsfWebHost**

CHAPTER 4.

15 (Fifteen) Special Keyboard Shortcuts.

The fifteen special keyboard shortcuts are fifteen (15) shortcuts every computer user should know.

The following is a list of keyboard shortcuts every computer user should know.

1. **Ctrl + A:** Control plus A, highlights or selects everything you have in the environment where you are working.

   *If you are like **"Wow, the content of this document is large and there is no time to select all of it, besides, it's going to mount pressure on my computer?"** Using the mouse for this is an outdated method of handling a task like selecting all, Ctrl+A will take care of that in a second.*

2. **Ctrl + C:** Control plus C copies any highlighted or selected element within the work environment.

   Saves the time and stress which would have been used to right click and click again just to copy. Use ctrl+c.

3. **Ctrl + N:** Control plus N opens a new window.

Instead of clicking **File, New, blank/ template** and another **click,** *just press **Ctrl + N*** and a fresh window will appear instantly.

4. **Ctrl + O:** Control plus O opens a new program.

    Use ctrl +O when you want to locate / open a file or program.

5. **Ctrl + P:** Control plus P prints the active document.

    Always use this to locate the printer dialog box, and thereafter print.

6. **Ctrl + S:** Control plus S saves a new document or file and changes made by the user.

    Please stop! Don't use the mouse. Just press Ctrl+S and everything will be saved.

7. **Ctrl +V:** Control plus V pastes copied elements into the active area of the program in use.

    Using ctrl+V in a case like this Saves the time and stress of right clicking and clicking again just to paste.

8. **Ctrl + W:** Control plus W is used to close the page you are working on when you want to leave the work environment.

    "There is a way Debby does this without using the mouse. Oh my God, why didn't I learn it then?" Don't worry, I have the answer. Debby presses Ctrl+W to close active windows.

9. **Ctrl + X:** Control plus X cuts elements (making the elements to disappear from their original place). The difference between cutting and deleting elements is that in Cutting, what was cut doesn't get lost permanently but prepares itself so that it can be pasted on another location selected by the user.

   *Use ctrl+x when you think **"this shouldn't be here and I can't stand the stress of retyping or redesigning it in the rightful place it belongs".***

10. **Ctrl + Y:** Control plus Y redoes an undone action.

    Ctrl+Z brought back what you didn't need? Press Ctrl+ Y to remove it again.

11. **Ctrl + Z:** Control plus Z undoes actions.
    Can't find what you typed now or a picture you inserted, it suddenly disappeared or you mistakenly removed it? Press Ctrl+Z to bring it back.

12. **Alt + F4:** Alternative plus F4 closes active windows or items.

    *You don't need to move the mouse in order to close an active window, just press **Alt + F4** if you are done or don't want somebody who is coming to see what you are doing.*

13. **Ctrl + F6:** Control plus F6 Navigates between open windows, making it possible for a user to see what is happening in windows that are active.

Are you working in Microsoft Word and want to find out if the other active window where your browser is loading a page is still progressing? Use Ctrl + F6.

14. **F1:** This displays the help window.

    *Is your computer malfunctioning? Use **F1** to find help when you don't know what next to do.*

15. **F12:** This enables user to make changes to an already saved document.

    F12 is the shortcut to use when you want to change the format in which you saved your existing document, password it, change its name, change the file location or destination, or make other changes to it. It will save your time.

CHAPTER 5.

Common Office for Mac Keyboard Shortcuts.

Here are common shortcuts you can use when working with your Mac computer.

Working With Files, Applications, And Tools

TASK	SHORTCUT
Create a new file or Outlook item	Command + N
Create a new file from a template or theme	SHIFT + Command + P
Expand or minimize the ribbon	Command + OPTION + R
Save	Command + S
Print	Command + P
Open a file	Command + O
Close a file	Command + W
Quit the current application	Command + Q
Hide the current application	Command + H
Hide other applications	OPTION + Command + H
Minimize the window	Command + M

Editing And Formatting

TASK	SHORTCUT

Undo the last change	Command + Z
Redo or repeat the last action	Command + Y
Cut the selection (and copy to clipboard)	Command + X
Copy the selection to the clipboard	Command + C
Copy the formatting from the selection	Command + SHIFT + C
Copy the selection to Scrapbook	CONTROL + OPTION + C
Paste	Command + V
Paste Special	Command + CONTROL + V
Paste the formatting to the selection	Command + SHIFT + V
Select All	Command + A
Find	Command + F
Insert hyperlink	Command + K

Dialog Boxes

TASK	SHORTCUT
Move to the next text box in a dialog box	TAB
Move to the previous box, option, control, or command in a dialog box	SHIFT + TAB
Exit a dialog box or cancel an action	ESC

Create A Custom Keyboard Shortcut For Office 2016 For Mac.

To create custom keyboard shortcuts in Office for Mac, use the built-in capability in Mac OS X.

1. From the **Apple** menu, click **System Preferences** > **Keyboard** > **Shortcuts** > **App Shortcuts**.
2. Click the + sign to add a keyboard shortcut.

3. In the **Application** menu, click the Office for Mac app (**Microsoft Excel**, **Microsoft Word**, **Microsoft PowerPoint**, **Microsoft OneNote**, **Microsoft Outlook**) you want to create keyboard a shortcut for.
4. Enter a **Menu Title** and the **Keyboard Shortcut** and click **Add**.

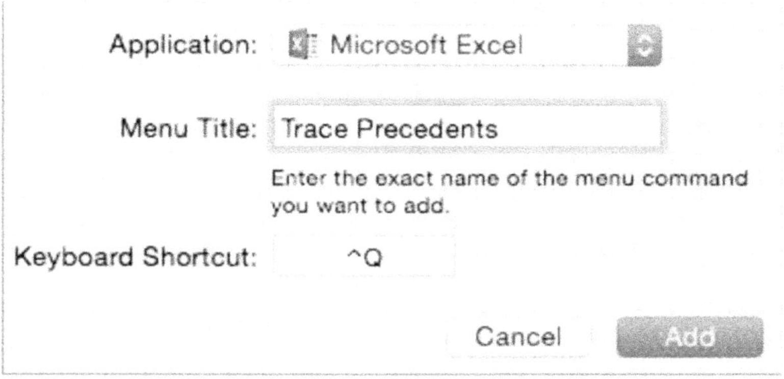

Application: Microsoft Excel

Menu Title: Trace Precedents

Enter the exact name of the menu command you want to add.

Keyboard Shortcut: ^Q

Cancel Add

Tip: If you aren't sure what the menu name is for a command, click **Help** in that app and search for what you want, which will then show you the exact menu name.

CHAPTER 6.

Keyboard Shortcuts In Word 2016 for Mac.

Definition of Program: Microsoft Word for Mac is a word processing program that goes with Ms. Office bundle or Office 365 subscription, designed by Microsoft Corporation. It allows users to create and modify simple and sophisticated documents.

The following list contains keyboard shortcuts that will boost your productivity in Microsoft Word 2016 for Mac.

Frequently Used Shortcuts

This table provides the frequently used shortcuts in Word 2016 for Mac.

TASK	SHORTCUT
Undo the last action	Command + Z or Control + Z
Cut selected text or graphics	Command + X or Control + X
Copy selected text or graphics to the Clipboard	Command + C or Control + C
Paste the Clipboard contents	Command+ V or Control + V
Choose the Go To command (Edit menu)	Option + Command + G
Open the Spelling and Grammar dialog box	Option + Command + L

Extend a selection	F8
Go to the next window	Command + Grave accent (`)
Choose the Save As command (File menu).	Command+ Shift + S
Copy selected text	Shift + F2
Change letters to uppercase, lowercase, or mixed case	Shift + F3
Find or Find and Replace	Control+F for Find; places the focus in the Search box Control+H for Find and Replace
Print a document	⌘+ P or Control + P
Move to the previous insertion point	Shift + F5
Go to the previous window	⌘+ Shift + `
Open the Thesaurus pane	Shift+ F7
Shrink a selection	Shift+ F8
Switch between a field code and its result	Shift + F9
Cut the selection to the Spike	Command+ F3
Close the window	Command+ F4
Expand or minimize the ribbon	Option + Command+ R
Edit a bookmark	Command+ Shift + F5
Find the next misspelling or grammatical error. The Check spelling as you type check box must be selected (Word menu, Preferences command, Spelling and Grammar).	Option + F7
Look up selected text on the Internet	Command+ Shift + L

Get Started

Many keyboards assign special functions to function keys, by default. To use the function key for other purposes, you have to press Fn+the function key.

Shortcut conflicts

Some Windows keyboard shortcuts conflict with the corresponding default Mac OS keyboard shortcuts. To use these shortcuts, you may have to change your Mac keyboard settings to change the Show Desktop shortcut for the key.

Change system preferences for keyboard shortcuts with the mouse

1. On the **Apple** menu, press **System Preferences.**
2. Click **Keyboard**.
3. Press the **Shortcuts** tab.
4. Click **Mission Control**.
5. Clear the check box for the keyboard shortcut that you want to use.

Move the Cursor

TASK	SHORTCUT
Move one character to the left	Left arrow
Move one character to the right	Right arrow
Move one word to the left	Option + Left arrow
Move one word to the right	Option + Right arrow
Move one paragraph up	Command+ Up arrow
Move one paragraph down	Command+ Down arrow
Move one cell to the left (in a table)	Shift + Tab

Move one cell to the right (in a table)	Tab
Move up one line	Up arrow
Move down one line	Down arrow
Move to the end of a line	Command+ Right arrow or End
Move to the beginning of a line	Command+ Left arrow or Home
Move up one screen (scrolling)	Page Up
Move down one screen (scrolling)	Page Down
Move to the top of the next page	Command+ Page Down
Move to the top of the previous page	Command+ Page Up
To the end of a document	Command+ End On a MacBook keyboard: Command+ FN + Right arrow
To the beginning of a document	Command+ Home On a MacBook keyboard: Command+ FN + Left arrow
To the previous insertion point	Shift + F5

Select Text And Graphics

Tip: If you know the key combination to move the cursor, you can generally select the text by using the same key combination while holding down Shift. For example,

Command+ Right arrow moves the cursor to the next word, and Command+ Shift + Right arrow selects the text from the cursor to the beginning of the next word.

TASK	SHORTCUT
Select multiple items not next to each other	Select the first item that you want, hold down Command, and then select any additional items
Select one character to the right	Shift + Right arrow
Select one character to the left	Shift + Left arrow
Select one word to the right	Shift + Option + Right arrow
Select one word to the left	Shift + Option + Left arrow
Select to the end of a line	Command+ Shift + Right arrow or Shift + End
Select to the beginning of a line	Command+ Shift + Left arrow or Shift + Home
Select one line down	Shift + Down arrow
Select one line up	Shift + Up arrow
Select to the end of a paragraph	Command+ Shift + Down arrow
Select to the beginning of a paragraph	Command+ Shift + Up arrow
Select one screen down	Shift + Page Down
Select one screen up	Shift + Page Up
Select to the beginning of a document	Command+ Shift + Home

Select to the end of a document	Command+ Shift + End
Select to the end of a window	Option + Command+ Shift + Page Down
Select to select the entire document	Command+ A
Select to a vertical block of text	Command+ Shift + F8 , and then use the arrow keys; press Esc to cancel selection mode
Select to a specific location in a document	F8 , and then use the arrow keys; press Esc to cancel selection mode

Select Text And Graphics In A Table

TASK	SHORTCUT
Select the next cell's contents	Tab
Select the preceding cell's contents	Shift + Tab
Extend a selection to adjacent cells	Hold down Shift and press an arrow key repeatedly
Select a column	Click in the column's top or bottom cell. Hold down Shift and press the Up arrow or Down arrow key repeatedly
Extend a selection (or block)	Command+ Shift + F8 , and then use the arrow keys; press Esc to cancel selection mode
Reduce the selection size	Shift + F8
Select multiple cells, columns, or rows that	Select the first item that you want, hold down Command, and then select any additional items

are not next to each other	

Extend a Selection

TASK	SHORTCUT
Turn on extend mode	F8 In extended selection mode, clicking a location in the document extends the current selection to that location.
Select the nearest character to the left	F8, Left arrow
Select the nearest character to the right	F8, Right arrow
Expand a selection	Press F8 repeatedly to expand the selection to the entire word, sentence, paragraph, section, and document.
Reduce the size of a selection	Shift + F8
Turn off extend mode	Esc

Edit Text and Graphics

TASK	SHORTCUT
Copy text or graphics	Command+ C or F3
Copy a style	Command+ Shift + C
Paste a style	Command+ Shift + V

Copy text or graphics to the Scrapbook	Control + Option + C
Cut selected text to the clipboard	Command+ X or F2
Move text or graphics	Command+ X or F2 (then move the cursor and press Command+ V or F4)
Create AutoText	Option + F3
Insert AutoText	Command+ Option + Shift + V
Paste the Clipboard contents	Command+ V or F4
Paste special	Command+ Control + V
Paste and match the formatting of the surrounding text	Command+ Option + Shift + V
Paste the Spike contents	Command+ Shift + F3
Delete one character to the left	Delete
Delete one word to the left	Command+ Delete
Delete one character to the right	Command or Clear
Delete one word to the right	Command+ Command
Cut selected text to the Clipboard	Command+ X or F2
Undo the last action	Command+ Z
Redo the last action	Command+ Y
Cut to the Spike	Command+ F3

Align and Format Paragraphs

TASK	SHORTCUT
Center a paragraph	Command+ E
Justify a paragraph	Command+ J

Left-align a paragraph	Command+ L
Right-align a paragraph	Command+ R
Indent a paragraph from the left	Control + Shift + M
Remove a paragraph indent from the left	Command+ Shift + M
Create a hanging indent	Command+ T
Remove a hanging indent	Command+ Shift + T
Start AutoFormat	Command+ Option + K
Apply the Normal style	Command+ Shift + N
Apply the Heading 1 style	Command+ Option + 1
Apply the Heading 2 style	Command+ Option + 2
Apply the Heading 3 style	Command+ Option + 3
Apply the List style when the cursor is at the beginning of a line	Command+ Shift + L
Insert a nonbreaking space	Option + Spacebar

Set Line Spacing

TASK	SHORTCUT
Set lines as single-spaced	Command+ 1
Set lines as double-spaced	Command+ 2
Set lines as 1.5-line spacing	Command+ 5
Add or remove one line of space directly preceding a paragraph	Command+ 0 (zero)

Format Characters

TASK	SHORTCUT
Change the font	Command+ Shift + F
Increase the font size	Command+ Shift + >
Decrease the font size	Command+ Shift + <
Increase the font size by 1 point	Command+]
Decrease the font size by 1 point	Command+ [
Change the formatting of characters (Font command, Format menu)	Command+ D
Change the case of letters	Shift + F3
Format in all capital letters	Command+ Shift + A
Apply bold formatting	Command+ B
Apply an underline	Command+ U
Underline words but not spaces	Command+ Shift + W
Double-underline text	Command+ Shift + D
Apply italic formatting	Command+ I
Format in all small capital letters	Command+ Shift + K
Apply subscript formatting (automatic spacing)	Command+ Equal sign
Apply superscript formatting (automatic spacing)	Command+ Shift + Plus sign
Apply strike-through formatting	Command+ Shift + X

Insert Special Characters

TASK	SHORTCUT
Insert an empty field	Command+ F9
Insert a line break	Shift + Return
Insert a page break	Command + Enter
Insert a column break	Command+ Shift + Return
Insert a nonbreaking hyphen	Command+ Shift + Hyphen
Insert the copyright symbol	Option + G
Insert the registered trademark symbol	Option + R
Insert the trademark symbol	Option + 2
Insert an ellipsis	Option + Semicolon

Work With Fields

TASK	SHORTCUT
Insert a DATE field	Control + Shift + D
Insert a LISTNUM field	Command + Option + Shift + L
Insert a PAGE field	Control + Shift + P
Insert a TIME field	Control + Shift + T
Insert an empty field	Command + F9
Update selected fields	F9
Unlink a field	Command+ Shift + F9
Switch between a field code and its result	Shift + F9
Switch between all field codes and their results	Option + F9

Run GOTOBUTTON or MACROBUTTON from the field that displays the field results	Option + Shift + F9
Go to the next field	F11
Go to the previous field	Shift + F11
Lock a field	Command+ F11
Unlock a field	Command+ Shift + F11

Outline a Document

TASK	SHORTCUT
Promote a paragraph	Control + Shift + Left arrow
Demote a paragraph	Control + Shift + Right arrow
Demote to body text	Command+ Shift + N
Move selected paragraphs up This keyboard shortcut conflicts with a default Mission Control key. To use this Office keyboard shortcut, you must first change the **Mission Control** shortcut for this key. On the Apple menu, click **System Preferences** > **Mission Control**. Under **Keyboard and Mouse**, choose another shortcut for **Mission Control**, or choose – (minus sign) to turn it off.	Control + Shift + Up arrow
Move selected paragraphs down This keyboard shortcut conflicts with a default Mission Control key. To use this	Control + Shift + Down arrow

Office keyboard shortcut, you must first change the **Application windows** shortcut for this key. On the Apple menu, click **System Preferences** > **Mission Control**. Under **Keyboard and Mouse**, choose another shortcut for **Application windows**, or choose – (minus sign) to turn it off.	
Expand text under a heading	Control + Shift + Plus sign
Collapse text under a heading	Control + Shift + Minus sign
Expand all body text and headings or collapse all body text	Control + Shift + A
Show the first line of body text or all body text	Control + Shift + L
Show all headings with the specified heading level	Control + Shift +<Heading level>

Review a Document

TASK	SHORTCUT
Insert a comment	Command+ Option + A
Turn track changes on or off	Command+ Shift + E
Go to the beginning of a comment	Home
Go to the end of a comment	End (The End key is not available on all keyboards)
Go to the beginning of the list of comments when in the Reviewing Pane	Command+ Home

Go to the end of the list of comments when in the Reviewing Pane	Command+ End

Print a Document

TASK	SHORTCUT
Print a document	Command+ P

Move Around in a Table

TASK	SHORTCUT
Move to the next cell	Tab (If the cursor is in the last cell of a table, pressing Tab adds a new row)
Move to the preceding cell	Shift + Tab
Move to the preceding or next row	Up arrow or Down arrow
Move to the first cell in the row	Control + Home
Move to the last cell in the row	Control + End
Move to the first cell in the column	Control + Page Up
Move to the last cell in the column	Control + Page Down
Start a new paragraph	Return
Add a new row at the bottom of the table	Tab at the end of the last row

Add text before a table at the beginning of a document	Return at the beginning of the first cell
Insert a row	Command+ Control + I

Resize Table Columns By Using The Ruler

TASK	SHORTCUT
Move a single column line Retain table width	Shift
Equally resize all columns to the right Retain table width	Command+ Shift
Proportionally resize all columns to the right Retain table width	Command

Resize Table Columns Directly In A Table

Tips:

- To display a column's measurements in the ruler when you resize the column, press Option with these shortcut keys.
- To finely adjust a column width, turn off snap-to functionality by pressing Option with the shortcut keys.

TASK	SHORTCUT
Move a single column line	No key

Retain table width	
Retain column sizes to the right Change table width	Shift
Equally resize all columns to the right Retain table width	Command+ Shift
Proportionally resize all columns to the right Retain table width	Command

Insert Paragraphs and Tab Characters in a Table

TASK	SHORTCUT
Insert a new paragraph in a cell	Return
Insert a Tab character in a cell	Option + Tab

Use Footnotes And Endnotes

TASK	SHORTCUT
Insert a footnote	Command+ Option + F
Insert an endnote	Command+ Option + E

Use Function Key Shortcuts

Word 2016 for Mac uses the function keys for common commands, including Copy and Paste. For quick access to these shortcuts, you can change your Apple system preferences so you don't have to press the Fn key every time you use a function key shortcut.

Note: Changing system function key preferences affects how the function keys work for your Mac, not just Word. After changing this setting, you can still perform the special features printed on a function key. Just press the Fn key. For example, to use the F12 key to change your volume, press Fn+F12.

Change function key preferences with the mouse

1. On the **Apple** menu, press **System Preferences**.
2. Select **Keyboard**.
3. On the **Keyboard** tab, select the check box for **Use all F1, F2, etc. keys as standard function keys**.

Function Key Shortcuts

TASK	SHORTCUT
Undo the last action	F1
Cut selected text or graphics	F2
Copy selected text or graphics to the clipboard	F3
Paste the Clipboard contents	F4
Choose the Go To command (Edit menu)	F5
Open the Spelling and Grammar dialog box	F7
Extend a selection	F8
Update selected fields.	F9
Go to the next window	Command + F6
Copy selected text	Shift + F2
Change letters to uppercase, lowercase, or mixed case	Shift + F3
Repeat a Find or Go To action	Shift + F4 or ⌘+ Shift + F4

Move to the previous insertion point	Shift + F5
Open the Thesaurus pane	Shift+ F7
Shrink a selection	Shift+ F8
Switch between a field code and its result.	Shift + F9
Go to the previous field. This keyboard shortcut conflicts with a default Mission Control key for **Show Desktop**. To use this Office keyboard shortcut, you must first change the **Show Desktop** shortcut for this key. On the Apple menu, click **System Preferences** > **Mission Control**. Under **Keyboard and Mouse**, choose another shortcut for **Show Desktop**, or choose – (minus sign) to turn it off.	Shift + F11
Cut the selection to the Spike	Command+ F3
Close the window	Command+ F4
Go to the next window	Command+ F6
Insert an empty field	Command+ F9
Lock a field	Command+ F11
Insert the contents of the Spike	Command+ Shift + F3
Edit a bookmark	Command+ Shift + F5
Update linked information in a Word source document	Command+ Shift + F7
Extend a selection as a block selection	Command+ Shift + F8, an arrow key
Unlink a field	Command+ Shift + F9
Unlock a field	Command+ Shift + F11
Create an AutoText entry	Option + F3

Find the next misspelling or grammatical error.	Option + F7
Run a macro	Option + F8
Switch between all field codes and their results	Option + F9
Look up selected text on the Internet	Command+ Shift + L
Run GOTOBUTTON or MACROBUTTON from the field that displays the field results	Option + Shift + F9

Create or delete a keyboard shortcut in Word 2016 for Mac.

You can create your own keyboard shortcuts to help you quickly do a task. However, if the keyboard shortcut is the same as a default Mac OS X keyboard shortcut, it won't work unless you turn off the Mac OS X keyboard shortcut.

Create a keyboard shortcut for a task

1. On the **Tools** menu, click **Customize Keyboard**.
2. In the **Categories** list, click a menu name.
3. In the **Commands** list, click the task that you want to assign a keyboard shortcut to.

   Any keyboard shortcuts that are currently assigned to the selected task appear in the **Current keys** box.

4. In the **Press new keyboard shortcut** box, type a key combination that includes at least one modifier key (⌘ + Option + F11).

If you type a keyboard shortcut that is already assigned, the action assigned to that key combination appears next to **Currently assigned to**.

5. Click **Assign**.

   Notes:

   - To cancel the keyboard shortcut assignment, press Esc.

Delete a keyboard shortcut for a task

Important: You can delete keyboard shortcuts that you added, but you can't delete the default keyboard shortcuts for Word.

1. On the **Tools** menu, click **Customize Keyboard**.
2. In the **Categories** list, click a menu name.
3. In the **Commands** list, click the task that you want to delete a keyboard shortcut from.
4. In the **Current keys** box, click the keyboard shortcut that you want to delete, and then click **Remove**.

Create a keyboard shortcut to insert a symbol

You can create a keyboard shortcut for a symbol, such as the telephone symbol from the Zapf Dingbats font (⌘+ Option + Shift + T.)

1. On the **Insert** tab, click **Advanced Symbol**.
2. Click the symbol or special character you want.
3. Click the symbol or character that you want.
4. Click **Keyboard Shortcut**.

5. In the **Press new keyboard shortcut** box, type a key combination that includes at least one modifier key (⌘ + Option + Shift + T.

   If you type a keyboard shortcut that is already assigned, the action assigned to that key combination appears next to **Currently assigned to**.

6. Click **Assign** and then click **OK**.

   Notes:

   - To cancel the keyboard shortcut assignment, press Esc.

7. Click **Cancel** to close the **Symbol** dialog box.

Delete a keyboard shortcut to insert a symbol

1. On the **Insert** menu, click **Symbol**.
2. Click the symbol or character that you want to delete a keyboard shortcut from.
3. Click **Keyboard Shortcut**.
4. In the **Current keys** box, click the keyboard shortcut that you want to delete, and then click **Remove**, and then click **OK**.
5. Click **Cancel** to close the **Symbol** dialog box.

Reset all keyboard shortcuts

1. On the **Tools** menu, click **Customize Keyboard**.
2. To restore keyboard shortcuts to their original state, click **Reset All**, and then in the confirmation message, click **Yes**.

Turn off a Mac OS X keyboard shortcut

To use a keyboard shortcut that is the same as a default Mac OS X keyboard shortcut, you must first turn off that Mac OS X keyboard shortcut.

1. On the **Apple** menu, click **System Preferences**.
2. Click **Keyboard**, and then click the **Shortcuts** tab.
3. Click through the categories to find a specific keyboard shortcut, and then for the one that you want to turn off, clear the check box.

CHAPTER 7.

Keyboard Shortcuts In OneNote 2016 for Mac.

Definition of Program: Microsoft OneNote 2016 for Mac is a program designed by Microsoft Corporation for effective note-taking by Macintosh computer users.

Frequently Used Shortcuts

The following table shows the most frequently used shortcuts in OneNote 2016 for Mac.

TASK	SHORTCUT
Select all items on the current page.	⌘+ A (Continue pressing to expand the scope of your selection.)
Select the page title.	⌘+ Shift + T
Cut the selected text or item.	⌘+ X
Copy the selected text or item to the clipboard.	⌘+ C
Paste the contents of the clipboard.	⌘+ V
Undo the last action.	⌘+ Z
Redo the last action.	⌘+ Y
Open notebook.	Shift+⌘ + O
Close notebook.	⌘+ W

Indent a paragraph from the left of a word.	Tab
Indent a paragraph from anywhere in a paragraph.	⌘+ Closing bracket ( ])
Remove a paragraph indent from the left.	Shift + Tab or ⌘+ Opening bracket ([ )
Zoom in	Shift + Tab or ⌘+ Plus sign (+)
Zoom out	Shift + Tab or ⌘+ Minus sign (-)
Reset zoom	⌘+ Zero (0)
Collapse an expanded outline.	Control + Shift + Plus sign (+)
Expand a collapsed outline.	Control + Shift + Minus sign (-)
Open a link.	Select link + Return
Copy the format of the selected text.	Option + ⌘+ C
Paste the copied text format to selected text.	Option + ⌘+ V
Start dictation	Fn + Fn
Insert emodi	Control + ⌘+ Space

Get Started

If a function key doesn't work as you expect it to, press the Fn key in addition to the function key. If you don't want to press the Fn key every time, you can change your Apple system preferences.

Change function key preferences with the mouse

1. On the **Apple** menu, press **System Preferences**.
2. Select **Keyboard**.

3. On the **Keyboard** tab, select the check box for **Use all F1, F2, etc** as standard function keys.

Change function key preferences with the keyboard

1. Press ⌘+ Spacebar. You hear "Spotlight System dialog," and you're instructed to type. Type sys and press Enter.
2. You hear "System Preferences." The focus is in the search window.
3. Type **a** and then press the Down arrow key until you hear "Accessibility, completion selected." Press Enter. The **Accessibility** dialog opens, allowing you to set preferences.
4. Press the Tab key until you hear "You are currently in a table."
5. Press the Down arrow key until you hear "Keyboard." Press the Tab key to move to the **Open Keyboard Preferences** button and press the Spacebar.
6. Press the Tab key until you hear "Use all F1, F2, etc. as standard function keys." The focus is on a check box. To select the check box, press the Spacebar.
7. To save your changes and close the dialog box, press ⌘ + Option + W.

Shortcut conflicts

Some Windows keyboard shortcuts conflict with the corresponding default Mac OS keyboard shortcuts. This topic flags such shortcuts with an asterisk. To use these shortcuts, you may have to change your Mac keyboard settings to change the Show Desktop shortcut for the key.

Change system preferences for keyboard shortcuts with the mouse

1. On the **Apple** menu, press **System Preferences**.

   Note: To use System Preferences, you must have full keyboard access turned on.

2. Press **Keyboard**
3. Press the **Shortcuts** tab.
4. Click **Mission Control**.
5. Clear the check box for the keyboard shortcut that you want to use.

If you need to perform this function with the keyboard, only please see the topic

Insert Content

TASK	SHORTCUT
Insert a line break without starting a new paragraph.	Shift + Return
Insert a line break.	Shift + Return
Insert the current date.	⌘+ D
Insert the current date and time.	⌘+ Shift + D
Insert equations (or convert selected text to a math equation).	Control + Equal sign (=)
Use Smart Lookup	Control + Option + ⌘+ L

Delete Content

TASK	SHORTCUT
Delete character to the left of cursor.	Delete

Delete character to the right of the cursor.	fn + Delete
Delete one word to the left.	Option + Delete
Delete one word to the right.	fn + Option +Delete or Option + Del

Move The Cursor

TASK	SHORTCUT
Move one character to the left.	Left Arrow
Move one character to the right.	Right Arrow
Move one word to the left.	Option +Left Arrow
Move up a line.	Up Arrow
Move down a line.	Down Arrow
Move to the beginning of the line.	⌘+ Left Arrow
Move to the end of the line.	⌘+ Right Arrow
Move to the beginning of the word to the left.	Option + Left Arrow
Move to the ending of the word to the right.	Option + Right Arrow
Go to next paragraph.	⌘+ Up Arrow
Go to previous paragraph.	⌘+ Down Arrow
Scroll up in the current page.	Page Up
Scroll down in the current page.	Page Down
Go to the top of the page.	Command + Up Arrow
Go to the bottom of the page.	Command + Down Arrow
Go to the next paragraph.	Option + Up Arrow
Go to the previous paragraph.	Option + Down Arrow

Format Tables

TASK	SHORTCUT
Create a table.	Tab
Create another column in a table with a single row.	Tab
Create another row when at the end cell of a table. NOTE: Press Return a second time to finish the table.	Return
Create a column to the right of the current column in a table.	⌘+ Option+ R
Create a column to the left of the current column in a table.	⌘+ Option + ECommand+Option+E didn't work for me.
Create a row below the current row in a table.	⌘+ Return
Create another paragraph in the same cell in a table.	Option + Return

Search

TASK	SHORTCUT
Search on the page.	⌘+ F
Search all notebooks.	⌘+ Option + F

Navigate Within a Notebook

TASK	SHORTCUT
Switch between sections in a notebook.	Option + Tab
Switch between pages in a section.	1. Start with the cursor within a page, then press Control + Tab. The focus moves to **Add Page**. 2. Press the Tab key to move the focus to your page. 3. Press the Up arrow key or Down arrow key to select the previous or next page in your section.
Move the selected paragraphs up.	⌘+ Shift + Up Arrow
Move the selected paragraphs down.	⌘+ Shift + Down Arrow
Move the selected paragraphs left (decreasing the indent).	⌘+ Shift + Left Arrow

Advanced Cursor Navigation

TASK	SHORTCUT
Move the insertion point up in the current page, or expand the page up.	⌘+ Option + Up Arrow
Move the insertion point down in the current page, or expand the page down.	⌘+ Option + Down Arrow

Move the insertion point left in the current page, or expand the page to the left.	⌘+ Option + Left Arrow
Move the insertion point right in the current page, or expand the page to the right.	⌘+ Option + Right Arrow

Other Commands

TASK	SHORTCUT
Open other notebooks or create new ones.	⌘+ O
View the list of your open notebooks.	Control + G
Create a new notebook page.	⌘+ N
Open the OneNote preferences.	⌘+ , (Comma)
Move page to another location.	⌘+ Shift + M
Copy page to another location.	⌘+ Shift + C
Move or copy page again to last selected section.	Option + ⌘+ T
Enter full-screen mode.	Control + ⌘ +_F
Synchronize this notebook.	⌘+ S
Synchronize all notebooks	Shift + ⌘+ S

CHAPTER 8.

Keyboard Shortcuts In Excel 2016 for Mac.

Definition of Program: Microsoft Excel for Mac is an electronic spreadsheet program developed and sold by Microsoft Corporation that enables its users to create, organize, format, and calculate data. It was first released for Macintosh in the year 1985 and later on released for Windows in 1987.

The following list contains keyboard shortcuts that will boost your productivity in Microsoft Excel 2016 for Mac.

Frequently Used Shortcuts

TASK	SHORTCUT
Paste	⌘+ V or CONTROL + V
Copy	⌘+ C or CONTROL + C
Clear	DELETE
Save	⌘+ S or CONTROL + S
Undo	⌘+ Z or CONTROL + Z

Redo	⌘+ SHIFT+ Z
Cut	⌘+ X or CONTROL + X
Bold	⌘+ B or CONTROL + B
Print	⌘+ P or CONTROL + P
Open Visual Basic	OPTION + F11
Fill Down	⌘+ D or CONTROL + D
Fill Right	⌘+ R or CONTROL + R
Insert cells	CONTROL + SHIFT + =
Delete cells	⌘+ HYPHEN or CONTROL + HYPHEN
Calculate all open workbooks	⌘+ = or F9
Close window	⌘+ W or CONTROL + W
Quit Excel	⌘+ Q
Display the **Go To** dialog box	CONTROL + G or F5

Display the **Format Cells** dialog box	⌘+ 1 or CONTROL + 1
Display the **Replace** dialog box	CONTROL + H or ⌘+ SHIFT + H
Paste Special	⌘+ OPTION + V
Underline	⌘+ U
Italic	⌘+ I or CONTROL + I
New blank workbook	⌘+ N or CONTROL + N
New workbook from template	⌘+ SHIFT + P
Display the **Save As** dialog box	⌘+ SHIFT + S or F12
Display the **Help** window	F1 or ⌘+ /
Select All	⌘+ SHIFT + SPACEBAR
Add or remove a filter	⌘+ SHIFT + F or CONTROL + SHIFT + L
Minimize or maximize the ribbon tabs	⌘+ OPTION + R
Display the **Open** dialog box	⌘+ O or CONTROL + O
Check spelling	F7
Open the thesaurus	SHIFT + F7
Display the **Formula Builder**	SHIFT + F3

Open the **Define Name** dialog box	⌘+ F3
Open the **Create names** dialog box	⌘+ SHIFT + F3
Insert a new sheet. **	SHIFT + F11

** This shortcut conflicts with a default Mac OS key assignment. To use this shortcut, you must change your Mac keyboard settings. Go to **Apple** > **System Preferences** > **Keyboard** > **Shortcuts**. Click **Mission Control**, and then click to deselect the **Show Desktop** option.

Function Keys

Note: If a function key doesn't work as you expect it to, press the **FN** key in addition to the function key. If you don't want to press the FN key each time, you can change your system preferences: Go to **Apple** > **System Preferences** > **Keyboard**. Then select the check box for **Use all F1, F2, etc. as standard function keys**.

TASK	SHORTCUT
Display the **Help** window	F1
Edit the selected cell	F2
Insert or edit a cell comment	SHIFT + F2
Open the **Save** dialog box	OPTION + F2
Open the Formula Builder	SHIFT + F3
Open the **Define Name** dialog box	⌘+ F3
Close	⌘+ F4
Display the **Go To** dialog box	F5
Display the **Find** dialog box	SHIFT + F5
Move to the **Search Sheet** box	CONTROL + F5
Check spelling	F7
Open thesaurus	SHIFT + F7

Extend the selection	F8
Add to the selection	SHIFT + F8
Display the **Macro** dialog box	OPTION + F8
Calculate all open workbooks.	F9
Calculate the active sheet	SHIFT + F9
Minimize the active window	CONTROL + F9
Display a contextual menu, or "right click" menu	SHIFT + F10
Maximize or restore the active window	CONTROL + F10 or ⌘+ F10
Insert a new chart sheet. **	F11
Insert a new sheet **	SHIFT + F11
Insert an Excel 4.0 macro sheet	⌘+ F11
Open Visual Basic	OPTION + F11
Display the **Save As** dialog box	F12
Display the **Open** dialog box	⌘+ F12

** This shortcut conflicts with a default Mac OS key assignment. To use this shortcut, you must change your Mac keyboard settings. Go to **Apple**> **System Preferences**> **Keyboard**> **Shortcuts**. Click **Mission Control**, and then click to deselect the **Show Desktop** option.

Move and Scroll in a Sheet or Workbook

TASK	SHORTCUT
Move one cell up, down, left, or right	An arrow key
Move to the edge of the current data region	⌘+ arrow key
Move to the beginning of the row	HOME

Move to the beginning of the sheet	CONTROL + HOME
Move to the last cell in use on the sheet	CONTROL + END
Move down one screen	PAGE DOWN On a MacBook, press FN + DOWN ARROW
Move up one screen	PAGE UP On a MacBook, press FN + UP ARROW
Move one screen to the right	OPTION + PAGE DOWN
Move one screen to the left	OPTION + PAGE UP
Move to the next sheet in the workbook	CONTROL + PAGE DOWN or OPTION + RIGHT ARROW
Move to the previous sheet in the workbook	CONTROL + PAGE DOWN or OPTION + LEFT ARROW
Scroll to display the active cell	CONTROL + DELETE
Display the **Go To** dialog box	CONTROL + G
Display the **Find** dialog box	CONTROL + F or SHIFT + F5
Access the **Search Sheet** box	⌘+ F
Move between unlocked cells on a protected sheet	TAB

Print

TASK	SHORTCUT

Print	⌘+ P or CONTROL + P
Print preview	⌘+ P or CONTROL + P

Enter Data on a Sheet

Note: If a function key doesn't work as you expect it to, press the **FN** key in addition to the function key. If you don't want to press the FN key each time, you can change your system preferences: Go to **Apple** > **System Preferences** > **Keyboard**. Then select the check box for **Use all F1, F2, etc. as standard function keys**.

TASK	**SHORTCUT**
Edit the selected cell	F2
Complete a cell entry and move forward in the selection	RETURN
Start a new line in the same cell	CONTROL + OPTION + RETURN
Fill the selected cell range with the text that you type	⌘+ RETURN or CONTROL + RETURN
Complete a cell entry and move up in the selection	SHIFT + RETURN
Complete a cell entry and move to the right in the selection	TAB
Complete a cell entry and move to the left in the selection	SHIFT + TAB
Cancel a cell entry	ESC

Delete the character to the left of the insertion point, or delete the selection	DELETE
Delete the character to the right of the insertion point, or delete the selection Note: Some smaller keyboards do not have this key	⌦
Delete text to the end of the line Note: Some smaller keyboards do not have this key	CONTROL + ⌦
Move one character up, down, left, or right	An arrow key
Move to the beginning of the line	HOME
Insert a comment	SHIFT + F2
Open and edit a cell comment	SHIFT + F2
Fill down	CONTROL + D or ⌘+ D
Fill to the right	CONTROL + R or ⌘+ R
Define a name	CONTROL + L

Work in Cells or the Formula Bar

Note: If a function key doesn't work as you expect it to, press the **FN** key in addition to the function key. If you don't want to press the FN key each time, you can change your system preferences: Go to **Apple** > **System Preferences** > **Keyboard**. Then select the check box for **Use all F1, F2, etc. as standard function keys**.

TASK	SHORTCUT
Edit the selected cell	F2
Edit the active cell and then clear it, or delete the preceding character in the active cell as you edit the cell contents	DELETE
Complete a cell entry	RETURN
Enter a formula as an array formula	⌘+ SHIFT + RETURN or CONTROL + SHIFT + RETURN
Cancel an entry in the cell or formula bar	ESC
Display the Formula Builder after you type a valid function name in a formula	CONTROL + A
Insert a hyperlink	⌘+ K or CONTROL + K
Edit the active cell and position the insertion point at the end of the line	CONTROL + U
Open the Formula Builder	SHIFT + F3
Calculate the active sheet	SHIFT + F9
Display a contextual menu	SHIFT + F10
Start a formula	=
Toggle the formula reference style between absolute, relative, and mixed	⌘+ T or F4
Insert the AutoSum formula	⌘+ SHIFT + T
Enter the date	CONTROL + SEMICOLON (;)
Enter the time	⌘+ SEMICOLON (;)

Copy the value from the cell above the active cell into the cell or the formula bar	CONTROL + SHIFT + INCH MARK (")
Alternate between displaying cell values and displaying cell formulas	CONTROL + GRAVE ACCENT (`)
Copy a formula from the cell above the active cell into the cell or the formula bar	CONTROL + APOSTROPHE (')
Display the AutoComplete list	CONTROL + OPTION + DOWN ARROW
Define a name	CONTROL + L
Open the **Smart Lookup** pane	CONTROL + OPTION + ⌘+ L

Format and Edit Data

TASK	SHORTCUT
Edit the selected cell	F2
Create a table	⌘+ T or CONTROL + T
Insert a line break in a cell	⌘+ OPTION + RETURN or CONTROL + OPTION + RETURN
Insert special characters like symbols, including Emoji	CONTROL + ⌘+ SPACEBAR
Increase font size	⌘+ SHIFT + >
Decrease font size	⌘+ SHIFT + <
Align center	⌘+ E
Align left	⌘+ L

Display the **Modify Cell Style** dialog box	⌘+ SHIFT + L
Display the **Format Cells** dialog box	⌘+ 1
Apply the general number format	CONTROL + SHIFT + ~
Apply the currency format with two decimal places (negative numbers appear in red with parentheses)	CONTROL + SHIFT + $
Apply the percentage format with no decimal places	CONTROL + SHIFT + %
Apply the exponential number format with two decimal places	CONTROL + SHIFT + ^
Apply the date format with the day, month, and year	CONTROL + SHIFT + #
Apply the time format with the hour and minute, and indicate A.M. or P.M.	CONTROL + SHIFT + @
Apply the number format with two decimal places, thousands separator, and minus sign (-) for negative values	CONTROL + SHIFT + !
Apply the outline border around the selected cells	⌘+ OPTION + ZERO
Add an outline border to the right of the selection	⌘+ OPTION + RIGHT ARROW
Add an outline border to the left of the selection	⌘+ OPTION + LEFT ARROW
Add an outline border to the top of the selection	⌘+ OPTION + UP ARROW
Add an outline border to the bottom of the selection	⌘+ OPTION + DOWN ARROW
Remove outline borders	⌘+ OPTION + HYPHEN
Apply or remove bold formatting	⌘+ B
Apply or remove italic formatting	⌘+ I
Apply or remove underscoring	⌘+ U

Apply or remove strikethrough formatting	⌘+ SHIFT + X
Hide a column	⌘+) or CONTROL +)
Unhide a column	⌘+ SHIFT +) or CONTROL + SHIFT +)
Hide a row	⌘+ (or CONTROL + (
Unhide a row	⌘+ SHIFT + (or CONTROL + SHIFT + (
Edit the active cell	CONTROL + U
Cancel an entry in the cell or the formula bar	ESC
Edit the active cell and then clear it, or delete the preceding character in the active cell as you edit the cell contents	DELETE
Paste text into the active cell	⌘+ V
Complete a cell entry	RETURN
Give selected cells the current cell's entry	⌘+ RETURN or CONTROL + RETURN
Enter a formula as an array formula	⌘+ SHIFT + RETURN or CONTROL + SHIFT + RETURN

Display the Formula Builder after you type a valid function name in a formula	CONTROL + A

Work With a Selection

TASK	SHORTCUT
Copy	⌘+ C or CONTROL + V
Paste	⌘+ V or CONTROL + V
Cut	⌘+ X or CONTROL + X
Clear	DELETE
Delete the selection	CONTROL + HYPHEN
Undo the last action	⌘+ Z
Hide a column	⌘+) or CONTROL +)
Unhide a column	⌘+ SHIFT +) or CONTROL + SHIFT +)
Hide a row	⌘+ (or CONTROL + (
Unhide a row	⌘+ SHIFT + (or CONTROL + SHIFT + (

Move from top to bottom within the selection (down) *	RETURN
Move from bottom to top within the selection (up) *	SHIFT + RETURN
Move from left to right within the selection, or move down one cell if only one column is selected	TAB
Move from right to left within the selection, or move up one cell if only one column is selected	SHIFT + TAB
Move clockwise to the next corner of the selection	CONTROL + PERIOD
Group selected cells	⌘+ SHIFT + K
Ungroup selected cells	⌘+ SHIFT + J

* These shortcuts may move in another direction other than down or up. If you'd like to change the direction of these shortcuts, click the **Excel** menu, and then click **Preferences**. Click **Edit**. Then change the direction for **After pressing Return, move selection**.

Select Cells, Columns, or Rows.

Note: If a function key doesn't work as you expect it to, press the **FN** key in addition to the function key. If you don't want to press the FN key each time, you can change your system preferences: Go to **Apple** > **System Preferences** > **Keyboard**. Then select the check box for **Use all F1, F2, etc. as standard function keys**.

TASK	SHORTCUT
Extend the selection by one cell	SHIFT + arrow key

Extend the selection to the last nonblank cell in the same column or row as the active cell	⌘+ SHIFT + arrow key
Extend the selection to the beginning of the row	SHIFT + HOME
Extend the selection to the beginning of the sheet	CONTROL + SHIFT + HOME
Extend the selection to the last cell used on the sheet (lower-right corner)	CONTROL + SHIFT + END
Select the entire column	CONTROL + SPACEBAR
Select the entire row	SHIFT + SPACEBAR
Select the entire sheet	⌘+ A
Select only visible cells	⌘+ SHIFT + * (asterisk)
Select only the active cell when multiple cells are selected	SHIFT + DELETE
Extend the selection down one screen	SHIFT + PAGE DOWN
Extend the selection up one screen	SHIFT + PAGE UP
Alternate between hiding objects, displaying objects, and displaying placeholders for objects	CONTROL + 6
Turn on the capability to extend a selection by using the arrow keys	F8
Add another range of cells to the selection	SHIFT + F8
Select the current array, which is the array that the active cell belongs to	CONTROL + /

Select cells in a row that don't match the value in the active cell in that row. You must select the row starting with the active cell	CONTROL + \
Select only cells that are directly referred to by formulas in the selection	CONTROL + SHIFT + [
Select all cells that are directly or indirectly referred to by formulas in the selection	CONTROL + SHIFT + {
Select only cells with formulas that refer directly to the active cell	CONTROL +]
Select all cells with formulas that refer directly or indirectly to the active cell	CONTROL + SHIFT + }

Use Charts

Note: If a function key doesn't work as you expect it to, press the **FN** key in addition to the function key. If you don't want to press the FN key each time, you can change your system preferences: Go to **Apple** > **System Preferences** > **Keyboard**. Then select the check box for **Use all F1, F2, etc. as standard function keys**.

TASK	SHORTCUT
Insert a new chart sheet. **	F11
Cycle through chart object selection	An arrow key

** This shortcut conflicts with a default Mac OS key assignment. To use this shortcut, you must change your Mac keyboard settings. Go to **Apple** > **System Preferences** >

Keyboard > **Shortcuts**. Click **Mission Control**, and then click to deselect the **Show Desktop** option.

Sort, Filter, and Use PivotTable Reports.

TASK	SHORTCUT
Open the **Sort** dialog box	⌘+ SHIFT + R
Add or remove a filter	⌘+ SHIFT + F or CONTROL + SHIFT + L
Display the Filter list or PivotTable page field pop-up menu for the selected cell	OPTION + DOWN ARROW

Outline Data

TASK	SHORTCUT
Display or hide outline symbols	CONTROL + 8
Hide selected rows	CONTROL + 9
Unhide selected rows	CONTROL + SHIFT + (
Hide selected columns	CONTROL + ZERO
Unhide selected columns	CONTROL + SHIFT +)

Work In Windows

Note: If a function key doesn't work as you expect it to, press the **FN** key in addition to the function key. If you don't want to press the FN key each time, you can change your system preferences: Go to **Apple** > **System Preferences** > **Keyboard**. Then select the check box for **Use all F1, F2, etc. as standard function keys**.

TASK	SHORTCUT
Expand or minimize the ribbon	⌘+ OPTION + R
Switch to full screen view	⌘+ CONTROL + F
Switch to the next application	⌘+ TAB
Switch to the previous application	⌘+ SHIFT + TAB
Close the active workbook window	⌘+ W
Copy the image of the screen and save it to a Screen Shot file on your desktop.	⌘+ SHIFT + 3
Minimize the active window	CONTROL + F9
Maximize or restore the active window	CONTROL + F10 or ⌘+ F10
Hide Excel.	⌘+ H

Work In Dialog Boxes

TASK	SHORTCUT
Move to the next text box	TAB
Move to the previous box, option, control, or command	SHIFT + TAB
Exit a dialog box or cancel an action	ESC
Perform the action assigned to the default command button (the button with the bold outline, often the **OK** button)	RETURN
Cancel the command and close	ESC

Use Function Key Shortcuts

Excel for Mac 2016 uses the function keys for common commands, including Copy and Paste. For quick access to these shortcuts, you can change your Apple system preferences so you don't have to press the Fn key every time you use a function key shortcut

Note: Changing system function key preferences affects how the function keys work for your Mac, not just Excel. After changing this setting, you can still perform the special features printed on a function key. Just press the Fn key. For example, to use the F12 key to change your volume, you would press Fn+F12.

If a function key doesn't work as you expect it to, press the **FN** key in addition to the function key. If you don't want to press the FN key each time, you can change your Apple system preferences:

Change function key preferences with the mouse

1. On the **Apple** menu, press **System Preferences**.
2. Select **Keyboard**.
3. On the **Keyboard** tab, select the check box for **Use all F1, F2, etc. keys as standard function keys**.

CHAPTER 9.

Keyboard Shortcuts In Outlook 2016 for Mac.

Definition of Program: Microsoft Outlook for Mac is an application designed by Microsoft Corporation that keeps people connected through its email services, and other powerful organizational tools.

The following list contains keyboard shortcuts that will boost your productivity in Microsoft Outlook 2016 for Mac.

Frequently Used Shortcuts

TASK	SHORTCUT
Save an item	⌘+ S
Print an item	⌘+ P
Undo the last action	⌘+ Z
Redo the last action	⌘+ Y
Minimize the active window	⌘+ M
Create a new folder in the navigation pane	Shift + ⌘+ N
Create new email (in Mail view)	⌘+ N
Hide the reading pane or show it on the right	⌘+ Backslash (\ )
Hide the reading pane or show it below	Shift + ⌘+ Backslash (\ )
Move the selected item to a different folder	Shift + ⌘+ M
Copy the selected item to a different folder	Shift + ⌘+ C

Select all items in the item list, if the item list is the active pane	⌘+ A
Minimize or expand the ribbon	Options + ⌘+ R
Hide Outlook	⌘+ H
Quit Outlook	⌘+ Q
Start dictation	Fn + Fn
Insert emoji	Control + ⌘+ Space

Work in Windows and Dialogs

TASK	SHORTCUT
Go to Mail view	⌘+ 1
Go to Calendar view	⌘+ 2
Go to Contacts view	⌘+ 3
Go to Tasks view	⌘+ 4
Go to Notes view	⌘+ 5
Open the Sync Status window or make it the active window	⌘+ 7
Open the Sync Errors or make it the active window	⌘+ 8
Open the Contacts Search window	⌘+ 0
Open the Outlook Preferences dialog box	⌘+ Comma (,)
Cycle forward through open windows	⌘+ Tilde (~)
Cycle back through open windows	Shift + ⌘+ Tilde (~)
Close the active window	⌘+ W
Open the selected item	⌘+ O
Move forward through controls in a window	Tab
Move back through controls in a window	Shift + Tab

Use Search

TASK	SHORTCUT
Search current folder	Option + ⌘+ F
Do an advanced search in Outlook (add Item Contains filter for searching)	Shift + ⌘+ F
Find text within an item	⌘+ F
Find the next instance of the text you searched for in an item	⌘+ G
Find the previous instance of the text you searched for in an item	⌘+ Shift + G

Send and Receive Mail

TASK	SHORTCUT
Create a new message	⌘+ N
Send the open message	⌘+ Return
Send all messages in the Outbox and receive all incoming messages	⌘+ K
Send all the messages in the Outbox	Shift + ⌘+ K
Save the open message and store it in the Drafts folder	⌘+ S
Add an attachment to the open message	⌘+ E
Open the Spelling and Grammar dialog box	⌘+ Colon (:)
Check recipient names in the open messages	Control + ⌘+ C
Reply to the sender of the message or, if the message is from a mailing list, reply to the mailing list	⌘+ R
Reply to all	Shift+ ⌘+ R
Forward the message	⌘+ J

Open the selected message in a separate window	⌘+ O
Clear the flag for the selected message	Option + ⌘+ Apostrophe (')
Mark the selected message as junk mail	⌘+ Shift + J
Mark the selected message as not junk mail	⌘+ Shift + Option + J
Display the previous message	Control + Opening bracket ([ )
Display the next message	Control + Closing bracket ( ])
Navigate to the previous pane in the Mail view	Shift + Control + Opening bracket ([ )
Navigate to the next pane in the Mail view	Shift + Control + Closing bracket ( ])
Move the selected message to a folder	Shift + ⌘+ M
Decrease the display size of text in an open message or in the reading pane	⌘+ Hyphen (-)
Increase the display size of text in an open message or in the reading pane	⌘+ Plus sign (+)
Scroll down to the next screen of text or, if you are at the end of a message, display the next message	Spacebar
Scroll up to the previous screen of text or, if you are at the beginning of a message, display the previous message	Shift+ Spacebar
Delete the selected message	Delete
Permanently delete the selected message	Shift + Delete
Delete the current message, and, if the message window is open, close it	⌘+ Delete
Mark selected messages as read	⌘+ T

Mark selected messages as unread	Shift + ⌘+ T
Mark all messages in a folder as read	Option + ⌘+ T

Use The Calendar

TASK	SHORTCUT
Open the Calendar window	⌘+ 2
Create a new appointment	⌘+ N
Open the selected calendar event	⌘+ O
Delete the calendar event	Delete
Switch the view to include today	⌘+ T
In Day view, move to the previous day. In Week and Work Week views, move to the previous week. In Month view, move to the previous month.	⌘+ Left arrow
In Day view, move to the next day. In Week and Work Week views, move to the next week. In Month view, move to the next month.	⌘+ Right arrow
Navigate to the previous pane in the Calendar view	Shift + Control + Opening bracket ([ )
Navigate to the next pane in the Calendar view	Shift + Control + Closing bracket ( ])

Work With People and Contacts

TASK	SHORTCUT
Create a new contact	⌘+ N
Open the selected contact	⌘+ O
Delete the contact	Delete

Close the current open contact and open the previous contact	Control + Opening bracket ([ )
Close the current open contact and open the next contact	Control + Closing bracket ( ])
Navigate to the previous pane in the People view	Shift+ Control + Opening bracket ([ )
Navigate to the next pane in the People view	Shift + Control + Closing bracket ( ])

Manage Tasks

TASK	SHORTCUT
Move to the Task window	⌘+ 4
Create a new task	⌘+ N
Open the selected task	⌘+ O
Delete the task	Delete
Close the current open task and open the previous task in the Tasks list	Control + Opening bracket ([ )
Close the current open task and open the next task in the Tasks list	Control + Closing bracket ( ])
Navigate to the previous pane in the Tasks view	Shift + Control + Opening bracket ([ )
Navigate to the next pane in the Tasks view	Shift + Control + Closing bracket ( ])

Use Notes

TASK	SHORTCUT
Move to the Notes window	⌘+ 5
Create a new note	⌘+ N
Open the selected note	⌘+ O

Delete the note	Delete
Close the current open note and open the previous note in the Notes list	Control + Opening bracket ([ )
Close the current open note and open the next note in the Notes list	Control + Closing bracket ( ])
Navigate to the previous pane in the Notes view	Shift + Control + Opening bracket ([ )
Navigate to the next pane in the Notes view	Shift + Control + Closing bracket ( ])
Send a note as an email	⌘+ J
Send a note as an HTML attachment to an email	Control + ⌘+ J First place the focus on the note in the list of notes.

Edit and Format Text

TASK	SHORTCUT
Cut the selected text to the clipboard	⌘+ X
Copy a selection to the clipboard	⌘+ C
Paste a selection from the clipboard	⌘+ V
Paste a selection from the clipboard and match the destination style	Shift + Option + ⌘+ V
Make the selected text bold	⌘+ B
Make the selected text italic	⌘+ I
Underline the selected text	⌘+ U

Strike through the selected text	Shift + ⌘+ X
Insert a hyperlink	Control + ⌘+ K
Move the cursor left one character	Left arrow
Move the cursor right one character	Right arrow
Move the cursor up one line	Up arrow
Move the cursor down one line	Down arrow
Move the cursor to the beginning of the current paragraph	Option + Up arrow
Move the cursor to the end of the current paragraph	Option + Down arrow
Move the cursor to the beginning of the current word	Option + Left arrow
Move the cursor to the end of the current word	Option + Right arrow
Decrease indent	⌦+ Opening brace ({)
Increase indent	⌦+ Closing brace ({)
Delete the character to the left of the cursor, or delete the selected text	Delete
Delete the character to the right side of the cursor, or delete the selected text	⌦ If your keyboard doesn't have a ⌦key, use FN + Delete.
Insert a tab stop	Tab
Move the cursor to the beginning of the line	⌘+ Left arrow
Move the cursor to the end of the line	⌘+ Right arrow

Move the cursor to the top of the message body	⌘+ Up arrow
Move the cursor to the bottom of the message body	⌘+ Down arrow
Move the cursor to the beginning of the selected text	⌘+ Home
Move the cursor to the end of the selected text	⌘+ End
Scroll up	Page up
Scroll down	Page down

Flag Messages, Contacts, and Tasks For Follow up

TASK	SHORTCUT
Flag the selected item for follow up, with Today as Due Date	Control + 1
Flag the selected item for follow up, with Tomorrow as Due Date	Control + 2
Flag the selected item for follow up, with This Week as Due Date	Control + 3
Flag the selected item for follow up, with Next Week as Due Date	Control + 4
Flag the selected item for follow up, with No Due Date	Control + 5
Flag the selected item for follow up, and add a custom Due Date	Control + 6
Flag the selected item for follow up, and add a reminder	Control + Equal sign (=)
Mark the selected item as Complete	Control + Zero (0)
Clear the selected item's follow-up flag	Option + ⌘+ Apostrophe (')

CHAPTER 10.

Keyboard Shortcuts In PowerPoint 2016 for Mac.

Definition of Program: Microsoft PowerPoint for Mac is a computer application used for graphic presentation that comes with Microsoft Office bundle, developed and sold by Microsoft Corporation.

This list contains keyboard shortcuts that will help you do your presentation better.

Editing Text and Objects

TASK	SHORTCUT
Delete one character to the left	DELETE
Delete one character to the right	FUNCTION + DELETE
Cut selected text or object	⌘+ X
Copy selected text or object	⌘+ C
Paste cut or copied text or object	⌘+ V
Paste special	⌘+ CONTROL + V
Increase the font size	⌘+ SHIFT + >
Decrease the font size	⌘+ SHIFT + <
Apply bold formatting	⌘+ B
Apply an underline	⌘+ U
Apply italic formatting	⌘+ I
Center a paragraph	⌘+ E
Justify a paragraph	⌘+ J
Left align a paragraph	⌘+ L

Right align a paragraph	⌘+ R
Redo the last action	⌘+ Y
Undo the last action	⌘+ Z
Open the Format Text dialog box, Font options	⌘+ T
Open the Format Text dialog box, Paragraph options	⌘+ OPTION + M

Moving Around in Text

TASK	SHORTCUT
To the beginning of a word or one word to the left	OPTION + LEFT ARROW
One word to the right	OPTION + RIGHT ARROW
To the end of a line	⌘+ RIGHT ARROW
To the beginning of a line	⌘+ LEFT ARROW
To the beginning of a paragraph or up one paragraph	OPTION + UP ARROW
Down one paragraph	OPTION + DOWN ARROW
To the start or end of all the text in the object you are editing	⌘+ UP/DOWN ARROW

Working With Objects

TASK	SHORTCUT
Select the next object	TAB
Select the previous object	SHIFT + TAB
Select all objects and all text	⌘+ A
Move the selected object in the direction of the arrow	Arrow keys or ⌘+ arrow key

Group the selected objects	⌘+ OPTION + G
Ungroup the selected objects	⌘+ OPTION + SHIFT + G
Regroup the selected objects	⌘+ OPTION + J
Rotate the selected object clockwise	OPTION + right arrow
Rotate the selected object counterclockwise	OPTION + left arrow
Format the selected object	⌘+ SHIFT + 1
Duplicate selected objects	⌘+ D
Resize selected objects	SHIFT + arrow keys

Presentations

TASK	SHORTCUT
Create a new presentation	⌘+ N
Create a new presentation with a template from the PowerPoint Presentation gallery	⌘+ SHIFT + P
Insert a new slide	CONTROL + M or ⌘+ SHIFT + N
Zoom out	⌘+ MINUS SIGN
Zoom in	⌘+ PLUS SIGN
Make a copy of the selected slide	⌘+ SHIFT + D
Open a presentation	⌘+ O
Close a presentation	⌘+ W
Print a presentation	⌘+ P
Save a presentation	⌘+ S
Save a presentation with a different name, location, or file format.	⌘+ SHIFT + S
Quit PowerPoint	⌘+ Q
Find text and formatting	⌘+ F
Add a hyperlink to selected text, an image, or an object	⌘+ K

Cancel a command, such as **Save As**	ESC
Undo an action	⌘+ Z
Redo or repeat an action	⌘+ Y
Move through multiple open presentations.	⌘+ ~
Open a recent file	⌘+ SHIFT+ O

Changing Views

TASK	**SHORTCUT**
Switch to normal view	⌘+ 1
Switch to slide sorter view	⌘+ 2
Switch to notes page view	⌘+ 3
Switch to outline view	⌘+ 4
Switch to slide show	⌘+ SHIFT + RETURN
Switch to full screen (hide menus)	⌘+ CONTROL + F
Switch to presenter view	OPTION + RETURN
Show or hide guides	⌘+ OPTION + CONTROL + G
Switch to handout master view	
Switch to slide master view	
Switch to notes master view	⌘+ OPTION + 3

Selecting Text

TASK	**SHORTCUT**
One character to the right	SHIFT + RIGHT ARROW
One character to the left	SHIFT + LEFT ARROW

From the insertion point to the same point one line up	SHIFT + UP ARROW
From the insertion point to the same point one line down	SHIFT + DOWN ARROW
All text to the start of the line	⌘+ SHIFT + LEFT ARROW
All text to the end of the line	⌘+ SHIFT + RIGHT ARROW
From the insertion point to the end of the paragraph	SHIFT + OPTION + DOWN ARROW
From the insertion point to the beginning of the paragraph	SHIFT + OPTION + UP ARROW

Slide Shows

You can use the following keyboard shortcuts while running your slide show in full-screen mode, with or without the presenter view.

Tip: You can press the / key during a slide show to see a list of keyboard shortcuts.

TASK	SHORTCUT
Perform the next animation or advance to the next slide	N , PAGE DOWN , RIGHT ARROW , DOWN ARROW , or the SPACEBAR (or click the mouse button)
Return to the previous animation or return to the previous slide	P , PAGE UP , LEFT ARROW , UP ARROW , or DELETE
Go to slide number	The number of the slide that you want to view, and then press RETURN

Display a black screen, or return to the slide show from a black screen	B or PERIOD
Display a white screen, or return to the slide show from a white screen	W or COMMA
Play slide show from the first slide	⌘+ SHIFT+ RETURN
Play slide show from the current slide	⌘+ RETURN
End a slide show	ESC , ⌘+ PERIOD , or HYPHEN
Erase on-screen annotations	E
Go to next hidden slide if the next slide is hidden	H
Redisplay hidden pointer and/or change the pointer to a pen	⌘+ P
Redisplay hidden pointer and/or change the pointer to an arrow	⌘+ A
Hide the pointer on mouse move	CONTROL + H
Display the contextual menu	Hold down CONTROL and click the mouse button
Show Thesaurus entry for a selected word	⌘+ OPTION + CONTROL + R
Show Smart Lookup entry for a selected word or phrase	⌘+ OPTION + CONTROL + L
Switch to presenter view	OPTION + RETURN

Working in Tables

TASK	SHORTCUT
Move to the next cell	TAB
Move to the preceding cell	SHIFT + TAB
Move to the next line or row	DOWN ARROW
Move to the preceding line or row	UP ARROW
Start a new paragraph in a cell	RETURN
Add a new row at the bottom of the table	TAB at the end of the last row

Windows and Dialog Boxes

TASK	SHORTCUT
Close the active window	⌘+ W
Perform the action assigned to a default button in a dialog box	RETURN
Cancel a command and close the dialog box	ESC
Hide the current window	⌘+ H
Minimize the current window	⌘+ M

CHAPTER 11.

Bonus Section

Safari 9 (El Capitan): Safari Keyboard and Other Shortcuts.

Safari is an internet browser developed by Apple Inc. that goes with Mac computers. It is fast and more energy efficient than any other browser as far as browsing with Macintosh computers are concerned.

This is a list of keyboard shortcuts you can use, in addition to those that appear in Safari menus.

Webpages

TASK	SHORTCUT
Scroll up, down, left, or right	Press the arrow keys.
Scroll in larger increments	Press Option while you press an arrow key.
Scroll down a screen	Page Down Space bar
Scroll up a screen	Page Up Shift–Space bar
Scroll to the top-left or bottom-left corner of the page	Command–Up Arrow or Home Command–Down Arrow or End

Highlight the next item on a webpage	Tab highlights the next text field or pop-up menu. Tab also highlights buttons and other controls if "All controls" is selected in the Shortcuts pane of the Keyboard pane of System Preferences. Option-Tab highlights the same items as Tab plus all other clickable items. To swap the behavior of Tab and Option-Tab, turn on "Press Tab to highlight each item on a webpage" in the Advanced pane of Safari preferences.
Open a page in a new tab	Command-click a link Command-click a bookmark Command-Return after typing in the Smart Search field.
Open a page in a new tab, and bring the tab to the front	Shift-Command-click a link Shift-Command-click a bookmark Shift-Command-Return after typing in the Smart Search field.
Bring the next tab to the front	Control-Tab or Shift-Command-]
Bring the previous tab to the front	Control-Shift-Tab or Shift-Command -[
Select one of your first nine tabs	Command-1 to Command-9
Close all tabs except for one	Option-click the close button (X) on the tab you want to leave open

Open in tabs all the bookmarks in a folder in the Favorites bar	Command-click the folder in the Favorites bar
See a list of recent pages by name	Hold down the Back or Forward button until the list appears
See a list of recent pages by web address (URL)	Press Option and hold down the Back or Forward button until the list appears
Go to your homepage	Command-Home key
While typing in the Smart Search field, restore the current webpage address	Esc
Close Reader	Esc
Exit full-screen view	Esc
Download a linked file	Option-click a link to the file
Open a downloaded file	Double-click the file in the downloads list

Reading List

TASK	SHORTCUT
Add the current page	Shift-Command-D
Add a linked page	Shift-click a link to the page
Remove a page	Swipe left over the page summary using a trackpad or mouse that supports gestures,

	then click Remove. Or, swipe all the way to the left until the page summary disappears.

Bookmarks

TASK	SHORTCUT
Add a bookmark to the Favorites bar	Click the Smart Search field to show the page's full address and its icon, then drag the icon to the Favorites bar
Move a bookmark on the Favorites bar	Drag the bookmark left or right
Remove a bookmark from the Favorites bar	Drag the bookmark off the top of the bar

Bookmarks Sidebar and Bookmarks View

TASK	SHORTCUT
Select bookmarks and folders in the sidebar	Command-click each bookmark and folder Shift-click to extend the selection
Select the next bookmark or folder	Up Arrow or Down Arrow
Open the selected bookmark	Space bar
Open the selected folder	Space bar or Right Arrow
Close the selected folder	Space bar or Left Arrow
Open the selected folder and its subfolders in the sidebar	Option–Right Arrow

Close the selected folder and its subfolders in the sidebar	Option–Left Arrow
Change the name or address of a bookmark	Select the bookmark, then press Return
Cancel editing a bookmark name in the sidebar	Esc
Finish editing a bookmark name	Return
Create a folder containing the selected bookmarks and folders in bookmarks view	Option-click the New Folder button at the bottom of the window
Delete a bookmark	Select the bookmark, then press Delete

Customer's Page.

This page is for customers who enjoyed Microsoft Office 365/2016 Keyboard Shortcuts For Macintosh.

Dearly beloved customer, please leave a review behind if you enjoyed this book or found it helpful. It will be highly appreciated, thank you.

Download Our Free EBooks Today.

In order to appreciate our customers, we have made some of our titles available at 0.00. Totally free. Feel free to get a copy of the free titles.

(A) For Keyboard Shortcuts In Windows

Go to Amazon: Windows 7 Keyboard shortcuts

Go to Other Stores: Windows 7 Keyboard Shortcuts

(B) For Keyboard Shortcuts In Office 2016

Go to Amazon: Word 2016 Keyboard Shortcuts For windows

Go to Other Stores: Word 2016 Keyboard Shortcuts For Windows

Note: Feel free to download them from your favorite store today. Thank you!

Other Books By This Publisher.

S/N	Title	Series
Series A: Limits Breaking Quotes.		
1	Discover Your Key Christian Quotes	Limits Breaking Quotes
Series B: Shortcut Matters.		
1	Windows 7 Shortcuts	Shortcut Matters
2	Windows 7 Shortcuts & Tips	Shortcut Matters
3	Windows 8.1 Shortcuts	Shortcut Matters
4	Windows 10 Shortcut Keys	Shortcut Matters
5	Microsoft Office 2007 Keyboard Shortcuts For Windows.	Shortcut Matters
6	Microsoft Office 2010 Shortcuts For Windows.	Shortcut Matters
7	Microsoft Office 2013 Shortcuts For Windows.	Shortcut Matters
8	Microsoft Office 2016 Shortcuts For Windows.	Shortcut Matters
Series C: Teach Yourself.		
1	Teach Yourself Computer Fundamentals	Teach Yourself
Series D: For Painless Publishing		
1	Self-Publish it with CreateSpace.	For Painless Publishing
2	Where is my money? Now solved for Kindle and CreateSpace	For Painless Publishing
3	Describe it on Amazon	For Painless Publishing
4	How To Market That Book.	For Painless Publishing